Hands-On Recommendation Systems with Python

Start building powerful and personalized, recommendation engines with Python

Rounak Banik

BIRMINGHAM - MUMBAI

Hands-On Recommendation Systems with Python

Copyright © 2018 Packt Publishing

Commissioning Editor: Pravin Dhandre
Acquisition Editor: Noyonika Das
Content Development Editor: Mohammed Yusuf Imaratwale
Technical Editor: Jinesh Topiwala
Copy Editor: Safis Editing
Project Coordinator: Hardik Bhinde
Proofreader: Safis Editing
Indexer: Priyanka Dhadke
Graphics: Jason Monteiro
Production Coordinator: Nilesh Mohite

First published: July 2018

Production reference: 2310718

Published by Packt Publishing Ltd.
Livery Place
35 Livery Street
Birmingham
B3 2PB, UK.

ISBN 978-1-78899-375-3

www.packtpub.com

To my mentor, Baran Toppare, and my friend, Utkarsh Bajpai, for their encouragement and support.

– Rounak Banik

`mapt.io`

Mapt is an online digital library that gives you full access to over 5,000 books and videos, as well as industry leading tools to help you plan your personal development and advance your career. For more information, please visit our website.

Why subscribe?

- Spend less time learning and more time coding with practical eBooks and Videos from over 4,000 industry professionals

- Improve your learning with Skill Plans built especially for you

- Get a free eBook or video every month

- Mapt is fully searchable

- Copy and paste, print, and bookmark content

PacktPub.com

Did you know that Packt offers eBook versions of every book published, with PDF and ePub files available? You can upgrade to the eBook version at `www.PacktPub.com` and as a print book customer, you are entitled to a discount on the eBook copy. Get in touch with us at `service@packtpub.com` for more details.

At `www.PacktPub.com`, you can also read a collection of free technical articles, sign up for a range of free newsletters, and receive exclusive discounts and offers on Packt books and eBooks.

Contributors

About the author

Rounak Banik is a Young India Fellow and an ECE graduate from IIT Roorkee. He has worked as a software engineer at Parceed, a New York start-up, and Springboard, an EdTech start-up based in San Francisco and Bangalore. He has also served as a backend development instructor at Acadview, teaching Python and Django to around 35 college students from Delhi and Dehradun.

He is an alumni of Springboard's data science career track. He has given talks at the SciPy India Conference and published popular tutorials on Kaggle and DataCamp.

I would like to thank Baran Toppare, my mentor for introducing and guiding me through the wonderfully exciting world of data science (and recommendation systems). I am also grateful to Parul Gupta and Indrajit Rajtilak, my former colleagues at Springboard. Without their support, I would not have pursued the Data Science Career Track and therefore, this book would never have been a reality.
Finally, I'd like to thank my family and all my friends in college for being a constant source of motivation, inspiration and support that enabled me to complete this book.

About the reviewer

Dr. S. Gowrishankar is currently working as associate professor in the department of computer science and engineering at Dr. Ambedkar Institute of Technology, Bengaluru, Karnataka, India. His current research interests are mainly focused on data science, including its technical aspects as well as its applications and implications. Specifically, he is interested in the applications of machine learning, data mining, and big data analytics in healthcare.

Image credits

Some of the images in the book are for illustrative purposes only. For more information refer to the links as follows:

- *Support Vector Machines Explained*, Tristan Fletcher (https://static1. squarespace.com/static/58851af9ebbd1a30e98fb283/t/ 58902fbae4fcb5398aeb7505/1485844411772/SVM+Explained.pdf
- *How Are Principal Component Analysis And Singular Value Decomposition Related?*, Andre Perunicic (https://intoli.com/blog/pca-and-svd/
- *Random Forest Classifier – Machine Learning, Balazs Holczer* (http://www. globalsoftwaresupport.com/random-forest-classifier-bagging-machine-learning/)
- *Machine Learning for Recommendation*, Dr. Rana Forsati (http://www.cse.msu. edu/~forsati/)
- *Approaches to analyse and interpret biological profile data*, Matthias Scholz (http:// phdthesis-bioinformatics-maxplanckinstitute-molecularplantphys. matthias-scholz.de/)
- *K Means*, Image Courtesy of Michael Jordan (http://stanford.edu/~cpiech/ cs221/handouts/kmeans.html)

Packt is searching for authors like you

If you're interested in becoming an author for Packt, please visit authors.packtpub.com and apply today. We have worked with thousands of developers and tech professionals, just like you, to help them share their insight with the global tech community. You can make a general application, apply for a specific hot topic that we are recruiting an author for, or submit your own idea.

Table of Contents

Preface

Recommendation systems are at the heart of almost every internet business today, from Facebook to Netflix to Amazon. Providing good recommendations, whether it's friends, movies, or groceries, goes a long way in defining user experience and enticing your customers to use and buy from your platform.

This book shows you how to do just that. You will learn about different kinds of recommenders used in the industry and see how to build them from scratch using Python. No need to wade through tons of linear algebra and machine learning theory, you'll get started with building and learning about recommenders as quickly as possible.

In this book, you will build an IMDB Top 250 clone, a content-based engine that works on movie metadata, collaborative filters that make use of customer behavior data, and a hybrid recommender that incorporates content-based and collaborative filtering techniques.

With this book, all you need to get started with building recommendation systems is familiarity with Python, and by the time you're finished, you will have a great grasp of how recommenders work, and you will be in a strong position to apply the techniques learned to your own problem domains.

Who this book is for

If you are a Python developer and want to develop applications for social networking, news personalization, or smart advertising, this is the book for you. Basic knowledge of machine learning techniques will be helpful, but it's not mandatory.

What this book covers

Chapter 1, *Getting Started with Recommender Systems*, introduces the recommendation problem and the models popularly used to solve it.

Chapter 2, *Manipulating Data with the Pandas Library*, illustrates various data wrangling techniques using the Pandas library.

Chapter 3, *Building an IMDB Top 250 Clone with Pandas*, walks through the process of building a top movies chart and a knowledge-based recommender that explicitly takes in user preferences.

Chapter 4, *Building Content-Based Recommenders*, describes the process of building models that make use of movie plot lines and other metadata to offer recommendations.

Chapter 5, *Getting Started with Data Mining Techniques*, covers various similarity scores, machine learning techniques, and evaluation metrics used to build and gauge performances of collaborative recommender models.

Chapter 6, *Building Collaborative Filters*, walks through the building of various collaborative filters that leverage user rating data to offer recommendations.

Chapter 7, *Hybrid Recommenders*, outlines various kinds of hybrid recommenders used in practice and walks you through the process of building a model that incorporates both content and collaborative-based filtering.

To get the most out of this book

This book will give you maximum benefit if you have some experience with Python development, or simply someone who wants to develop applications for social networking, news personalization, or smart advertising, this is the book for you. Having some knowledge of **machine learning** (**ML**) techniques will be helpful, but it is not mandatory.

Download the example code files

You can download the example code files for this book from your account at www.packtpub.com. If you purchased this book elsewhere, you can visit www.packtpub.com/support and register to have the files emailed directly to you.

You can download the code files by following these steps:

1. Log in or register at www.packtpub.com.
2. Select the **SUPPORT** tab.
3. Click on **Code Downloads & Errata**.
4. Enter the name of the book in the **Search** box and follow the onscreen instructions.

Once the file is downloaded, please make sure that you unzip or extract the folder using the latest version of:

- WinRAR/7-Zip for Windows
- Zipeg/iZip/UnRarX for Mac
- 7-Zip/PeaZip for Linux

The code bundle for the book is also hosted on GitHub
at `https://github.com/PacktPublishing/Hands-On-Recommendation-Systems-with-Python`. In case there's an update to the code, it will be updated on the existing GitHub
repository.

We also have other code bundles from our rich catalog of books and videos available
at `https://github.com/PacktPublishing/`. Check them out!

Download the color images

We also provide a PDF file that has color images of the screenshots/diagrams used in this
book. You can download it here:
`http://www.packtpub.com/sites/default/files/downloads/HandsOnRecommendationSyst
emswithPython_ColorImages.pdf`.

Code in action

Visit the following link to check out videos of the code being run:

`http://bit.ly/2JV4oeu`.

Conventions used

There are a number of text conventions used throughout this book.

`CodeInText`: Indicates code words in text, database table names, folder names, filenames,
file extensions, pathnames, dummy URLs, user input, and Twitter handles. Here is an
example: "Let's now implement the SVD filter using the `surprise` package."

A block of code is set as follows:

```
#Import SVD
from surprise import SVD

#Define the SVD algorithm object
svd = SVD()

#Evaluate the performance in terms of RMSE
evaluate(svd, data, measures=['RMSE'])
```

When we wish to draw your attention to a particular part of a code block, the relevant lines or items are set in bold:

```
else:
        #Default to a rating of 3.0 in the absence of any information
        wmean_rating = 3.0
    return wmean_rating
score(cf_user_wmean)
```

OUTPUT:
1.0174483808407588

Any command-line input or output is written as follows:

```
sudo pip3 install scikit-surprise
```

Bold: Indicates a new term, an important word, or words that you see onscreen. For example, words in menus or dialog boxes appear in the text like this. Here is an example: "We see that the u.user file contains demographic information about our users, such as their **age**, **sex**, **occupation**, and **zip_code**."

Warnings or important notes appear like this.

Tips and tricks appear like this.

Get in touch

Feedback from our readers is always welcome.

General feedback: Email feedback@packtpub.com and mention the book title in the subject of your message. If you have questions about any aspect of this book, please email us at questions@packtpub.com.

Errata: Although we have taken every care to ensure the accuracy of our content, mistakes do happen. If you have found a mistake in this book, we would be grateful if you would report this to us. Please visit www.packtpub.com/submit-errata, selecting your book, clicking on the Errata Submission Form link, and entering the details.

Piracy: If you come across any illegal copies of our works in any form on the Internet, we would be grateful if you would provide us with the location address or website name. Please contact us at copyright@packtpub.com with a link to the material.

If you are interested in becoming an author: If there is a topic that you have expertise in and you are interested in either writing or contributing to a book, please visit authors.packtpub.com.

Reviews

Please leave a review. Once you have read and used this book, why not leave a review on the site that you purchased it from? Potential readers can then see and use your unbiased opinion to make purchase decisions, we at Packt can understand what you think about our products, and our authors can see your feedback on their book. Thank you!

For more information about Packt, please visit packtpub.com.

Getting Started with Recommender Systems

Almost everything we buy or consume today is influenced by some form of recommendation; whether that's from friends, family, external reviews, and, more recently, from the sources selling you the product. When you log on to Netflix or Amazon Prime, for example, you will see a list of movies and television shows the service thinks you will like based on your past watching (and rating) history. Facebook suggests people it thinks you may know and would probably like to add. It also curates a News Feed for you based on the posts you've liked, the people you've be-friended, and the pages you've followed. Amazon recommends items to you as you browse for a particular product. It shows you similar products from a competing source and suggests auxiliary items *frequently bought together* with the product.

So, it goes without saying that providing a good recommendation is at the core of successful business for these companies. It is in Netflix's best interests to engage you with content that you love so that you continue to subscribe to its service; the more relevant the items Amazon shows you, the greater your chances – and volume – of purchases will be, which directly translates to greater profits. Equally, establishing *friendship* is key to Facebook's power and influence as an almost omnipotent social network, which it then uses to churn money out of advertising.

In this introductory chapter, we will acquaint ourselves with the world of recommender systems, covering the following topics:

- What is a recommender system? What can it do and not do?
- The different types of recommender systems

Technical requirements

You will be required to have Python installed on a system. Finally, to use the Git repository of this book, the user needs to install Git.

The code files of this chapter can be found on GitHub:
`https://github.com/PacktPublishing/Hands-On-Recommendation-Systems-with-Python`.

Check out the following video to see the code in action:

`http://bit.ly/2JTtg6t`.

What is a recommender system?

Recommender systems are pretty self-explanatory; as the name suggests, they are systems or techniques that recommend or suggest a particular product, service, or entity. However, these systems can be classified into the following two categories, based on their approach to providing recommendations.

The prediction problem

In this version of the problem, we are given a matrix of m users and n items. Each row of the matrix represents a user and each column represents an item. The value of the cell in the ith row and the jth column denotes the rating given by user i to item j. This value is usually denoted as r_{ij}.

For instance, consider the matrix in the following screenshot:

	i_1	i_2	i_3	i_4	i_5	i_6
U1	4	?	3	?	5	?
U2	?	2	?	?	4	1
U3	?	?	1	?	2	5
U4	?	?	3	?	?	1
U5	1	4	?	?	2	5
U6	5	?	2	1	?	4
U7	?	2	3	?	4	5

This matrix has seven users rating six items. Therefore, m = 7 and n = 6. User 1 has given the item 1 a rating of 4. Therefore, r_{11} = 4.

Let us now consider a more concrete example. Imagine you are Netflix and you have a repository of 20,000 movies and 5,000 users. You have a system in place that records every rating that each user gives to a particular movie. In other words, you have the rating matrix (of shape 5,000 × 20,000) with you.

However, all your users will have seen only a fraction of the movies you have available on your site; therefore, the matrix you have is sparse. In other words, most of the entries in your matrix are empty, as most users have not rated most of your movies.

The prediction problem, therefore, aims to predict these missing values using all the information it has at its disposal (the ratings recorded, data on movies, data on users, and so on). If it is able to predict the missing values accurately, it will be able to give great recommendations. For example, if user *i* has not used item *j*, but our system predicts a very high rating (denoted by $\hat{r}_{ij}$), it is highly likely that *i* will love *j* should they discover it through the system.

The ranking problem

Ranking is the more intuitive formulation of the recommendation problem. Given a set of n items, the ranking problem tries to discern the top k items to recommend to a particular user, utilizing all of the information at its disposal.

Imagine you are Airbnb, much like the preceding example. Your user has input the specific things they are looking for in their host and the space (such as their location, and budget). You want to display the top 10 results that satisfy those aforementioned conditions. This would be an example of the ranking problem.

It is easy to see that the prediction problem often boils down to the ranking problem. If we are able to predict missing values, we can extract the top values and display them as our results.

In this book, we will look at both formulations and build systems that effectively solve them.

Types of recommender systems

In recommender systems, as with almost every other machine learning problem, the techniques and models you use (and the success you enjoy) are heavily dependent on the quantity and quality of the data you possess. In this section, we will gain an overview of three of the most popular types of recommender systems in decreasing order of data they require to inorder function efficiently.

Collaborative filtering

Collaborative filtering leverages the power of community to provide recommendations. Collaborative filters are one of the most popular recommender models used in the industry and have found huge success for companies such as Amazon. Collaborative filtering can be broadly classified into two types.

User-based filtering

The main idea behind user-based filtering is that if we are able to find users that have bought and liked similar items in the past, they are more likely to buy similar items in the future too. Therefore, these models recommend items to a user that similar users have also liked. Amazon's *Customers who bought this item also bought* is an example of this filter, as shown in the following screenshot:

Imagine that Alice and Bob mostly like and dislike the same video games. Now, imagine that a new video game has been launched on the market. Let's say Alice bought the game and loved it. Since we have discerned that their tastes in video games are extremely similar, it's likely that Bob will like the game too; hence, the system recommends the new video game to Bob.

Item-based filtering

If a group of people have rated two items similarly, then the two items must be similar. Therefore, if a person likes one particular item, they're likely to be interested in the other item too. This is the principle on which item-based filtering works. Again, Amazon makes good use of this model by recommending products to you based on your browsing and purchase history, as shown in the following screenshot:

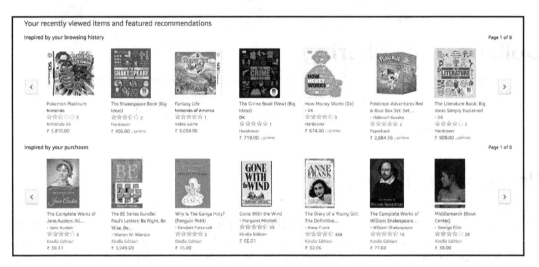

Item-based filters, therefore, recommend items based on the past ratings of users. For example, imagine that Alice, Bob, and Eve have all given *War and Peace* and *The Picture of Dorian Gray* a rating of excellent. Now, when someone buys *The Brothers Karamazov*, the system will recommend *War and Peace* as it has identified that, in most cases, if someone likes one of those books, they will like the other, too.

Shortcomings

One of the biggest prerequisites of a collaborative filtering system is the availability of data of past activity. Amazon is able to leverage collaborative filters so well because it has access to data concerning millions of purchases from millions of users.

Therefore, collaborative filters suffer from what we call the **cold start problem**. Imagine you have started an e-commerce website – to build a good collaborative filtering system, you need data on a large number of purchases from a large number of users. However, you don't have either, and it's therefore difficult to build such a system from the start.

Content-based systems

Unlike collaborative filters, content-based systems do not require data relating to past activity. Instead, they provide recommendations based on a user profile and metadata it has on particular items.

Netflix is an excellent example of the aforementioned system. The first time you sign in to Netflix, it doesn't know what your likes and dislikes are, so it is not in a position to find users similar to you and recommend the movies and shows they have liked.

As shown in the previous screenshot, what Netflix does instead is ask you to rate a few movies that you *have* watched before. Based on this information and the metadata it already has on movies, it creates a watchlist for you. For instance, if you enjoyed the *Harry Potter* and *Narnia* movies, the content-based system can identify that you like movies based on fantasy novels and will recommend a movie such as *Lord of the Rings* to you.

However, since content-based systems don't leverage the power of the community, they often come up with results that are not as impressive or relevant as the ones offered by collaborative filters. In other words, content-based systems usually provide recommendations that are *obvious*. There is little novelty in a *Lord of the Rings* recommendation if *Harry Potter* is your favorite movie.

Knowledge-based recommenders

Knowledge-based recommenders are used for items that are very rarely bought. It is simply impossible to recommend such items based on past purchasing activity or by building a user profile. Take real estate, for instance. Real estate is usually a once-in-a-lifetime purchase for a family. It is not possible to have a history of real estate purchases for existing users to leverage into a collaborative filter, nor is it always feasible to ask a user their real estate purchase history.

In such cases, you build a system that asks for certain specifics and preferences and then provides recommendations that satisfy those aforementioned conditions. In the real estate example, for instance, you could ask the user about their requirements for a house, such as its locality, their budget, the number of rooms, and the number of storeys, and so on. Based on this information, you can then recommend properties that will satisfy all of the above conditions.

Knowledge-based recommenders also suffer from the problem of low novelty, however. Users know full-well what to expect from the results and are seldom taken by surprise.

Hybrid recommenders

As the name suggests, hybrid recommenders are robust systems that combine various types of recommender models, including the ones we've already explained. As we've seen in previous sections, each model has its own set of advantages and disadvantages. Hybrid systems try to nullify the disadvantage of one model against an advantage of another.

Let's consider the Netflix example again. When you sign in for the first time, Netflix overcomes the cold start problem of collaborative filters by using a content-based recommender, and, as you gradually start watching and rating movies, it brings its collaborative filtering mechanism into play. This is far more successful, so most practical recommender systems are hybrid in nature.

In this book, we will build a recommender system of each type and will examine all of the advantages and shortcomings described in the previous sections.

Summary

In this chapter, we gained an overview of the world of recommender systems. We saw two approaches to solving the recommendation problem; namely, prediction and ranking. Finally, we examined the various types of recommender systems and discussed their advantages and disadvantages.

In the next chapter, we will learn to process data with pandas, the data analysis library of choice in Python. This, in turn, will aid us in building the various recommender systems we've introduced.

Manipulating Data with the Pandas Library 2

In the next few portions of the book, we are going to get our hands dirty by building the various kinds of recommender systems that were introduced in chapter one. However, before we do so, it is important that we know how to handle, manipulate, and analyze data efficiently in Python.

The datasets we'll be working with will be several megabytes in size. Historically, Python has never been well-known for its speed of execution. Therefore, analyzing such huge amounts of data using vanilla Python and the built-in data structures it provides us is simply impossible.

In this chapter, we're going to get ourselves acquainted with the pandas library, which aims to overcome the aforementioned limitations, making data analysis in Python extremely efficient and user-friendly. We'll also introduce ourselves to the *Movies Dataset* that we're going to use to build our recommenders as well as use pandas to extract some interesting facts and narrate the history of movies using data.

Disclaimer:
If you are already familiar with the pandas library, you may skip this chapter and move on to the next, *Building an IMDB Top 250 Clone with pandas*.

Technical requirements

You will be required to have Python installed on a system. Finally, to use the Git repository of this book, the user needs to install Git.

The code files of this chapter can be found on GitHub:
https://github.com/PacktPublishing/Hands-On-Recommendation-Systems-with-Python.

Check out the following video to see the code in action:

http://bit.ly/2LoZEUj.

Setting up the environment

Before we start coding, we should probably set up our development environment. For data scientists and analysts using Python, the Jupyter Notebook is, by far, the most popular tool for development. Therefore, we strongly advise that you use this environment.

We will also need to download the pandas library. The easiest way to obtain both is to download Anaconda. Anaconda is a distribution that comes with the Jupyter software and the SciPy packages (which includes pandas).

 You can download the distribution here: https://www.anaconda.com/download/.

The next step is to create a new folder (I'm going to name it RecoSys) in your desired location. This will be the master folder that contains all the code we write as part of this book. Within this folder, create another folder named Chapter2, which will contain all the code we write as part of this chapter.

Next, open your Terminal application, navigate to the Chapter2 folder, and run the jupyter notebook command. The commands should look something like this if you're on a Mac or Linux (the cd path will differ in Windows):

```
[rounakbanik:~]$ cd RecoSys/Chapter2
[rounakbanik:~/RecoSys/Chapter2]$ jupyter notebook
```

Jupyter Notebooks run on the browser on the localhost. Therefore, they're OS-independent. In other words, the experience will be the same regardless of whether you're on a Mac, a PC, or a Linux box.

Upon running the `jupyter notebook` command, your default browser should open up to the `localhost:8888/tree` URL and a window that looks as follows:

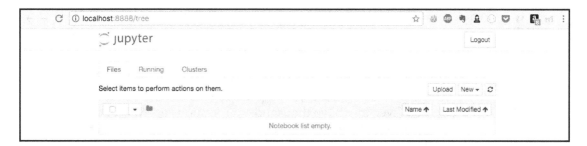

To the right of the window, you should be able to see a **New** dropdown. Click it and create a new Python 3 (or Python 2) Notebook. Doing so will open a new tab with an untitled notebook. You'll also be able to see an input cell with a pointer in it. This is space where we write our code (and markdown). Go ahead and type the following lines:

```
import pandas as pd
pd.__version__
```

To execute the code in this cell, press *Shift + Enter*. If all goes well, you should see a new output cell, which prints the version of the pandas library (for us, it is 0.20.3):

```
In [1]:  import pandas as pd
         pd.__version__

Out[1]:  '0.20.3'

In [ ]:
```

Congratulations!

You've now successfully set up your development environment. Of course, there is much more to Jupyter Notebooks than running a cell. We will be talking about these other features as and when we use them. Since this is not a book on Jupyter, we will be redirecting you to the free tutorials online if you're interested in learning the fundamentals of the Jupyter Notebook first. DataCamp has a definitive article on the subject.

 You can find the DataCamp Jupyter Notebook Tutorial here: `https://www.datacamp.com/community/tutorials/tutorial-jupyter-notebook`.

 In case you're having trouble setting up your environment, googling the error should direct you to a page suggesting a suitable solution. Websites such as Stack Overflow have thousands of questions on Anaconda setup and it is extremely likely that the problem you're facing has been faced by someone else before.

The Pandas library

Pandas is a package that gives us access to high-performance, easy-to-use tools and data structures for data analysis in Python.

As we stated in the introduction, Python is a slow language. Pandas overcomes this by implementing heavy optimization using the C programming language. It also gives us access to Series and DataFrame, two extremely powerful and user-friendly data structures imported from the R Statistical Package.

Pandas also makes importing data from external files into the Python environment a breeze. It supports a wide variety of formats, such as JSON, CSV, HDF5, SQL, NPY, and XLSX.

As a first step toward working with pandas, let's import our movies data into our Jupyter Notebook. To do this, we need the path to where our dataset is located. This can be a URL on the internet or your local computer. We highly recommend downloading the data to your local computer and accessing it from a local path instead of from a web URL.

 Go to the following URL to download the required CSV file: `https://www.kaggle.com/rounakbanik/the-movies-dataset/downloads/movies_metadata.csv/7`.

Create a new folder called `data` in the `RecoSys` directory and move the `movies_metadata.csv` file that you just downloaded into this folder. Now, let's witness some pandas magic. In the Jupyter Notebook you ran in the previous section, go to the second cell and type the following code:

```
#Read the CSV File into df
df = pd.read_csv('../data/movies_metadata.csv')

#We will find out what the following code does a little later!
df.head()
```

Et voila! You should be able to see a table-like structure with five rows, each row representing a movie. You can also see that the table has 24 columns, although the columns were truncated to fit in the display.

What is this structure though? Let's find out by running the familiar `type` command:

```
#Output the type of df
type(df)
```

You should get an output stating that df is a `pandas.core.frame.DataFrame`. In other words, our code has read the CSV file into a pandas DataFrame object. But what are DataFrames? Let's find that out in the next section.

The Pandas DataFrame

As we saw in the previous section, the `df.head()` code outputted a table-like structure. In essence, the DataFrame is just that: a two-dimensional data structure with columns of different data types. You can think of it as an SQL Table. Of course, just being a table of rows and columns isn't what makes the DataFrame special. The DataFrame gives us access to a wide variety of functionality, some of which we're going to explore in this section.

Each row in our DataFrame represents a movie. But how many movies are there? We can find this out by running the following code:

```
#Output the shape of df
df.shape

OUTPUT:
(45466, 24)
```

The result gives us the number of rows and columns present in df. We can see that we have data on 45,466 movies.

We also see that we have 24 columns. Each column represents a feature or a piece of metadata about the movie. When we ran df.head(), we saw that most of the columns were truncated to fit in the display. To view all the columns (henceforth, called features) we have, we can run the following:

```
#Output the columns of df
df.columns
```

OUTPUT:

```
Index(['adult', 'belongs_to_collection', 'budget', 'genres', 'homepage',
'id',
        'imdb_id', 'original_language', 'original_title', 'overview',
        'popularity', 'poster_path', 'production_companies',
        'production_countries', 'release_date', 'revenue', 'runtime',
        'spoken_languages', 'status', 'tagline', 'title', 'video',
        'vote_average', 'vote_count'],
      dtype='object')
```

We see that we have a lot of information on these movies, including their title, budget, genres, release date, and revenue.

Next, let's find out how to access a particular movie (or row). The first way to do this is by using the .iloc method. This allows us to select rows based on the numeric position, starting from zero. For example, if we wanted to access the second movie in the DataFrame, we'd run:

```
#Select the second movie in df
second = df.iloc[1]
second
```

The output will give you information about the movie on each of its 24 features. We see that the title of the movie is *Jumanji* and that it was released on December 15th, 1995, among other things.

 A cell will always print the output of the last line of code. Therefore, we don't need to explicitly write it within a print function.

The second way to do it is by accessing the DataFrame index. Since we didn't explicitly set an index while reading the CSV file, pandas defaulted it to zero-based indexing. We can change the index of df quite easily. Let's change the index to the title of the movie and try to access Jumanji using this index:

```
#Change the index to the title
df = df.set_index('title')

#Access the movie with title 'Jumanji'
jum = df.loc['Jumanji']
jum
```

You should see an output identical to the previous cell. Let's revert back to our zero-based numeric index:

```
#Revert back to the previous zero-based indexing
df = df.reset_index()
```

It is also possible to create a new, smaller DataFrame with fewer columns. Let's create a new DataFrame that only has the following features: title, release_date, budget, revenue, runtime, and genres:

```
#Create a smaller dataframe with a subset of all features
small_df = df[['title', 'release_date', 'budget', 'revenue', 'runtime',
'genres']]

#Output only the first 5 rows of small_df
small_df.head()
```

You should see a table with five movies and only the features that we've mentioned. The .head() method simply displays the first five rows of the DataFrame. You can display as many rows as you want by passing it as an argument into .head():

```
#Display the first 15 rows
small_df.head(15)
```

Next, let's check out the data types of our various features:

```
#Get information of the data types of each feature
small_df.info()
```

```
OUTPUT:
<class 'pandas.core.frame.DataFrame'>
RangeIndex: 45466 entries, 0 to 45465
Data columns (total 6 columns):
title 45460 non-null object
release_date 45379 non-null object
```

```
budget 45466 non-null object
revenue 45460 non-null float64
runtime 45203 non-null float64
genres 45466 non-null object
dtypes: float64(2), object(4)
memory usage: 2.1+ MB
```

A curious observation here is that pandas correctly deciphers `revenue` and `runtime` as float data, but assigns the generic object data type to `budget`.

However, pandas allows us to manually convert the data type of a feature. Let's try to convert the `budget` feature to `float`:

```python
#Convert budget to float
df['budget'] = df['budget'].astype('float')
```

```
OUTPUT:
...
...
ValueError: could not convert string to float:
'/zaSf5OG7V8X8gqFvly88zDdRm46.jpg'
```

Running this cell throws `ValueError`. It is easy to guess that one of the budget fields had a `'/zaSf...'` string as its value, and pandas was not able to convert this into a floating number.

To solve this problem, we will use the `apply()` method. This will allow us to apply a function to every field in a particular column and convert it into the return value. We are going to convert every number field in `budget` to float and, if that fails, convert it to `NaN`:

```python
#Import the numpy library
import numpy as np

#Function to convert to float manually
def to_float(x):
    try:
        x = float(x)
    except:
        x = np.nan
    return x

#Apply the to_float function to all values in the budget column
small_df['budget'] = small_df['budget'].apply(to_float)

#Try converting to float using pandas astype
small_df['budget'] = small_df['budget'].astype('float')
```

```
#Get the data types for all features
small_df.info()
```

This time around, there are no errors thrown. Also, we notice that the `budget` feature is now of the `float64` type.

Now, let's try to define a new feature, called `year`, that represents the year of release. The recommended way to do this would be by using the `datetime` functionality that pandas gives us:

```
#Convert release_date into pandas datetime format
small_df['release_date'] = pd.to_datetime(small_df['release_date'],
errors='coerce')

#Extract year from the datetime
small_df['year'] = small_df['release_date'].apply(lambda x: str(x).split('-
')[0] if x != np.nan else np.nan)

#Display the DataFrame with the new 'year' feature
small_df.head()
```

What are the oldest movies available in this dataset? To answer this question, we can sort the DataFrame based on the year of release:

```
#Sort DataFrame based on release year
small_df = small_df.sort_values('year')

small_df.head()
```

We see that we have movies from as early as the 1870s, with *Passage of Venus* being the oldest movie on record. Next, let's find out the most successful movies of all time. To do this, we'll use the `sort_values()` method once again, but with an additional `ascending=False` parameter to sort `DataFrame` in descending order:

```
#Sort Movies based on revenue (in descending order)
small_df = small_df.sort_values('revenue', ascending=False)

small_df.head()
```

From our results, we observe that *Avatar* is the most successful movie of all time, with a revenue of over $2.78 billion.

Let's say we wanted to create a new DataFrame of movies that satisfied a certain condition. For instance, we only want movies that earned more than $1 billion. Pandas makes this possible using its Boolean Indexing feature. Let's see this in action:

```
#Select only those movies which earned more than 1 billion
new = small_df[small_df['revenue'] > 1e9]
new
```

It is also possible to apply multiple conditions. For instance, let's say we only wanted movies that earned more than $1 billion, but where the outlay less than $150 million, we'd do it as follows:

```
#Select only those movies which earned more than 1 billion and spent less
than 150 million

new2 = small_df[(small_df['revenue'] > 1e9) & (small_df['budget'] < 1.5e8)]
new2
```

Only four movies make it into this list.

There is, of course, much more to what you can do with DataFrames (such as handling missing data), but we'll stop our exploration with it for now. Let's move on to another data structure we have unknowingly used extensively in this section: the Pandas Series.

The Pandas Series

When we accessed the Jumanji movie using `.loc` and `.iloc`, the data structures returned to us were Pandas Series objects. You may have also noticed that we were accessing entire columns using `df[column_name]`. This, too, was a Pandas Series object:

```
type(small_df['year'])
```

OUTPUT:
pandas.core.series.Series

The Pandas Series is a one-dimensional labelled array capable of holding data of any type. You may think of it as a Python list on steroids. When we were using the `.apply()` and `.astype()` methods in the previous section, we were actually using them on these Series objects.

Therefore, like the DataFrame, the Series object comes with its own group of extremely useful methods that make data analysis a breeze.

First, let's check out the shortest- and longest-running movies of all time. We will do this by accessing the `runtime` column of the DataFrame as a Series object and applying its methods on it:

```
#Get the runtime Series object
runtime = small_df['runtime']

#Print the longest runtime of any movie
print(runtime.max())

#Print the shortest runtime of any movie
print(runtime.min())
```

We see that the longest movie is more than 1,256 minutes in length and the shortest is 0! Of course, such strange results demand a deeper inspection of the data but we shall skip that, for now.

It is also possible to calculate the mean and median of the Series in this way. Let's do so for the movie budgets:

```
#Get the budget Series object
budget = small_df['budget']

#Print the mean budget of the movies
print(budget.mean())

#Print the median budget of the movies
print(budget.median())
```

The average budget of a movie is $4.2 million and the median budget is 0! This suggests that at least half the movies in our dataset have no budget at all! Like in the previous case, such strange results demand closer inspection. In this case, it is highly likely that a zero budget indicates that the data is not available.

What is the revenue that the 90th-percentile movie generated? We can discover this using the `quantile` function:

```
#Get the revenue Series object
revenue = small_df['revenue']

#Revenue generated by the 90th percentile movie
revenue.quantile(0.90)
```

We get a result of $8.26 million. What this means is that only 10% of the movies in our dataset earned more than $8.26 million in revenue.

Finally, let's find out the number of movies released each year. We do this using the `value_counts()` method on the `year` series:

```
#Get number of movies released each year
small_df['year'].value_counts()
```

We have the highest number of movies released in 2014. There are also six years in our dataset (including 2020) that have only one movie on record.

We'll stop our tour of the pandas library here. As I have already mentioned, there is much more to pandas than what we have covered in this chapter. However, this should be sufficient to tackle the data-wrangling and analysis tasks that we'll encounter while building our recommenders.

You may rename the notebook as `Chapter2` by clicking on **Untitled** and then close it. For the next chapter, we will create a new notebook.

Summary

In this chapter, we gained an understanding of the limitations of using vanilla Python and its built-in data structures. We acquainted ourselves with the Pandas library and learned how it overcomes the aforementioned difficulties by giving us access to extremely powerful and easy-to-use data structures. We then explored the two main data structures, Series and DataFrame, by analyzing our movies-metadata dataset.

In the next chapter, we will use our newfound skills to build an IMDB Top 250 Clone and its variant, a type of knowledge-based recommender.

3
Building an IMDB Top 250 Clone with Pandas

The **Internet Movie Database (IMDB)** maintains a chart called the IMDB Top 250, which is a ranking of the top 250 movies according to a certain scoring metric. All the movies in this list are non-documentary, theatrical releases with a runtime of at least 45 minutes and over 250,000 ratings:

This chart can be considered the simplest of recommenders. It doesn't take into consideration the tastes of a particular user, nor does it try to deduce similarities between different movies. It simply calculates a score for every movie based on a predefined metric and outputs a sorted list of movies based on that score.

In this chapter, we will be covering the following:

- Building a clone of the IMDB Top 250 chart (henceforth referred to as the simple recommender).
- Taking the functionalities of the chart one step further and building a knowledge-based recommender. This model takes user preferences with regards to genre, timeframe, runtime, language, and so on, and recommends movies that satisfy all conditions.

Technical requirements

You will be required to have Python installed on a system. Finally, to use the Git repository of this book, the user needs to install Git.

The code files of this chapter can be found on GitHub:
https://github.com/PacktPublishing/Hands-On-Recommendation-Systems-with-Python.

Check out the following video to see the code in action:

http://bit.ly/2v7SZD4.

The simple recommender

The first step in building our simple recommender is setting up our workspace. Let's create a new directory named Chapter3. Create a Jupyter Notebook in this directory named Simple Recommender and open it in the browser.

Let's now load the dataset we used in the previous chapter into our notebook.

In case you have not downloaded it already, the dataset is available at `https://www.kaggle.com/rounakbanik/the-movies-dataset/downloads/movies_metadata.csv/7`.

```
import pandas as pd
import numpy as np

#Load the dataset into a pandas dataframe
df = pd.read_csv('../data/movies_')

#Display the first five movies in the dataframe
df.head()
```

Upon running the cell, you should see a familiar table-like structure output in the notebook.

Building the simple recommender is fairly straightforward. The steps are as follows:

1. Choose a metric (or score) to rate the movies on
2. Decide on the prerequisites for the movie to be featured on the chart
3. Calculate the score for every movie that satisfies the conditions
4. Output the list of movies in decreasing order of their scores

The metric

The metric is the numeric quantity based on which we rank movies. A movie is considered to be better than another movie if it has a higher metric score than the other movie. It is very important that we have a robust and a reliable metric to build our chart upon to ensure a good quality of recommendations.

The choice of a metric is arbitrary. One of the simplest metrics that can be used is the movie rating. However, this suffers from a variety of disadvantages. In the first place, the movie rating does not take the popularity of a movie into consideration. Therefore, a movie rated 9 by 100,000 users will be placed below a movie rated 9.5 by 100 users.
This is not desirable as it is highly likely that a movie watched and rated only by 100 people caters to a very specific niche and may not appeal as much to the average person as the former.

It is also a well-known fact that as the number of voters increase, the rating of a movie normalizes and it approaches a value that is reflective of the movie's quality and popularity with the general populace. To put it another way, movies with very few ratings are not very reliable. A movie rated 10/10 by five users doesn't necessarily mean that it's a good movie.

Therefore, what we need is a metric that can, to an extent, take into account the movie rating and the number of votes it has garnered (a proxy for popularity). This would give a greater preference to a blockbuster movie rated 8 by 100,000 users over an art house movie rated 9 by 100 users.

Fortunately, we do not have to brainstorm a mathematical formula for the metric. As the title of this chapter states, we are building an IMDB top 250 clone. Therefore, we shall use IMDB's weighted rating formula as our metric. Mathematically, it can be represented as follows:

$$\textit{Weighted Rating (WR)} = (\frac{v}{v+m} \times R) + (\frac{m}{v+m} \times C)$$

The following apply:

- v is the number of votes garnered by the movie
- m is the minimum number of votes required for the movie to be in the chart (the prerequisite)
- R is the mean rating of the movie
- C is the mean rating of all the movies in the dataset

We already have the values for v and R for every movie in the form of the `vote_count` and `vote_average` features respectively. Calculating C is extremely trivial, as we have already seen in the previous chapter.

The prerequisties

The IMDB weighted formula also has a variable m, which it requires to compute its score. This variable is in place to make sure that only movies that are above a certain threshold of popularity are considered for the rankings. Therefore, the value of m determines the movies that qualify to be in the chart and also, by being part of the formula, determines the final value of the score.

Just like the metric, the choice of the value of *m* is arbitrary. In other words, there is no right value for *m*. It is a good idea to experiment with different values of *m* and then choose the one that you (and your audience) think gives the best recommendations. The only thing to be kept in mind is that the higher the value of *m*, the higher the emphasis on the popularity of a movie, and therefore the higher the selectivity.

For our recommender, we will use the number of votes garnered by the 80th percentile movie as our value for *m*. In other words, for a movie to be considered in the rankings, it must have garnered more votes than at least 80% of the movies present in our dataset. Additionally, the number of votes garnered by the 80th percentile movie is used in the weighted formula described previously to come up with the value for the scores.

Let us now calculate the value of *m*:

```
#Calculate the number of votes garnered by the 80th percentile movie
m = df['vote_count'].quantile(0.80)
m
```

OUTPUT:
50.0

We can see that only 20% of the movies have gained more than 50 votes. Therefore, our value of *m* is 50.

Another prerequisite that we want in place is the runtime. We will only consider movies that are greater than 45 minutes and less than 300 minutes in length. Let us define a new DataFrame, q_movies, which will hold all the movies that qualify to appear in the chart:

```
#Only consider movies longer than 45 minutes and shorter than 300 minutes
q_movies = df[(df['runtime'] >= 45) & (df['runtime'] <= 300)]

#Only consider movies that have garnered more than m votes
q_movies = q_movies[q_movies['vote_count'] >= m]

#Inspect the number of movies that made the cut
q_movies.shape
```

OUTPUT:
(8963, 24)

We see that from our dataset of 45,000 movies approximately 9,000 movies (or 20%) made the cut.

Calculating the score

The final value that we need to discover before we calculate our scores is C, the mean rating for all the movies in the dataset:

```
# Calculate C
C = df['vote_average'].mean()
C
```

OUTPUT:
5.6182072151341851

We can see that the average rating of a movie is approximately 5.6/10. It seems that IMDB happens to be particularly strict with their ratings. Now that we have the value of C, we can go about calculating our score for each movie.

First, let us define a function that computes the rating for a movie, given its features and the values of m and C:

```
# Function to compute the IMDB weighted rating for each movie
def weighted_rating(x, m=m, C=C):
    v = x['vote_count']
    R = x['vote_average']
    # Compute the weighted score
    return (v/(v+m) * R) + (m/(m+v) * C)
```

Next, we will use the familiar `apply` function on our `q_movies` DataFrame to construct a new feature score. Since the calculation is done for every row, we will set the axis to 1 to denote row-wise operation:

```
# Compute the score using the weighted_rating function defined above
q_movies['score'] = q_movies.apply(weighted_rating, axis=1)
```

Sorting and output

There is just one step left. We now need to sort our DataFrame on the basis of the score we just computed and output the list of top movies:

	title	vote_count	vote_average	score	runtime
10309	Dilwale Dulhania Le Jayenge	661.0	9.1	8.855148	190.0
314	The Shawshank Redemption	8358.0	8.5	8.482863	142.0
834	The Godfather	6024.0	8.5	8.476278	175.0
40251	Your Name.	1030.0	8.5	8.366584	106.0
12481	The Dark Knight	12269.0	8.3	8.289115	152.0
2843	Fight Club	9678.0	8.3	8.286216	139.0
292	Pulp Fiction	8670.0	8.3	8.284623	154.0
522	Schindler's List	4436.0	8.3	8.270109	195.0
23673	Whiplash	4376.0	8.3	8.269704	105.0
5481	Spirited Away	3968.0	8.3	8.266628	125.0
2211	Life Is Beautiful	3643.0	8.3	8.263691	116.0
1178	The Godfather: Part II	3418.0	8.3	8.261335	200.0
1152	One Flew Over the Cuckoo's Nest	3001.0	8.3	8.256051	133.0
1176	Psycho	2405.0	8.3	8.245381	109.0
351	Forrest Gump	8147.0	8.2	8.184252	142.0
1184	Once Upon a Time in America	1104.0	8.3	8.183804	229.0
1154	The Empire Strikes Back	5998.0	8.2	8.178656	124.0
18465	The Intouchables	5410.0	8.2	8.176357	112.0
289	Leon: The Professional	4293.0	8.2	8.170276	110.0
3030	The Green Mile	4166.0	8.2	8.169381	189.0
1170	GoodFellas	3211.0	8.2	8.160414	145.0
2216	American History X	3120.0	8.2	8.159278	119.0
1161	12 Angry Men	2130.0	8.2	8.140785	96.0
9698	Howl's Moving Castle	2049.0	8.2	8.138499	119.0
2884	Princess Mononoke	2041.0	8.2	8.138264	134.0

And voila! You have just built your very first recommender. Congratulations!

We can see that the Bollywood film *Dilwale Dulhania Le Jayenge* figures at the top of the list. We can also see that it has a noticeably smaller number of votes than the other Top 25 movies. This strongly suggests that we should probably explore a higher value of *m*. This is left as an exercise for the reader; experiment with different values of *m* and observe how the movies in the chart change.

The knowledge-based recommender

In this section, we are going to go ahead and build a knowledge-based recommender on top of our IMDB Top 250 clone. This will be a simple function that will perform the following tasks:

1. Ask the user for the genres of movies he/she is looking for
2. Ask the user for the duration
3. Ask the user for the timeline of the movies recommended
4. Using the information collected, recommend movies to the user that have a high weighted rating (according to the IMDB formula) and that satisfy the preceding conditions

The data that we have has information on the duration, genres, and timelines, but it isn't currently in a form that is directly usable. In other words, our data needs to be wrangled before it can be put to use to build this recommender.

In our `Chapter3` folder, let's create a new Jupyter Notebook named `Knowledge Recommender`. This notebook will contain all the code that we write as part of this section.

As usual, let us load our packages and the data into our notebook. Let's also take a look at the features that we have and decide on the ones that will be useful for this task:

```
import pandas as pd
import numpy as np

df = pd.read_csv('../data/movies_metadata.csv')

#Print all the features (or columns) of the DataFrame
df.columns
```

OUTPUT:
Index(['adult', 'belongs_to_collection', 'budget', 'genres', 'homepage', 'id',
        'imdb_id', 'original_language', 'original_title', 'overview',
        'popularity', 'poster_path', 'production_companies',
        'production_countries', 'release_date', 'revenue', 'runtime',

```
    'spoken_languages', 'status', 'tagline', 'title', 'video',
    'vote_average', 'vote_count'],
  dtype='object')
```

From our output, it is quite clear which features we do and do not require. Now, let's reduce our DataFrame to only contain features that we need for our model:

```
#Only keep those features that we require
df = df[['title','genres', 'release_date', 'runtime', 'vote_average',
'vote_count']]

df.head()
```

Next, let us extract the year of release from our `release_date` feature:

```
#Convert release_date into pandas datetime format
df['release_date'] = pd.to_datetime(df['release_date'], errors='coerce')

#Extract year from the datetime
df['year'] = df['release_date'].apply(lambda x: str(x).split('-')[0] if x
!= np.nan else np.nan)
```

Our `year` feature is still an `object` and is riddled with `NaT` values, which are a type of null value used by Pandas. Let's convert these values to an integer, 0, and convert the datatype of the `year` feature into `int`.

To do this, we will define a helper function, `convert_int`, and apply it to the `year` feature:

```
#Helper function to convert NaT to 0 and all other years to integers.
def convert_int(x):
    try:
        return int(x)
    except:
        return 0

#Apply convert_int to the year feature
df['year'] = df['year'].apply(convert_int)
```

We do not require the `release_date` feature anymore. So let's go ahead and remove it:

```
#Drop the release_date column
df = df.drop('release_date', axis=1)

#Display the dataframe
df.head()
```

The `runtime` feature is already in a form that is usable. It doesn't require any additional wrangling. Let us now turn our attention to `genres`.

Genres

Upon preliminary inspection, we can observe that the genres are in a format that looks like a JSON object (or a Python dictionary). Let us take a look at the `genres` object of one of our movies:

```
#Print genres of the first movie
df.iloc[0]['genres']
```

OUTPUT:
```
"[{'id': 16, 'name': 'Animation'}, {'id': 35, 'name': 'Comedy'}, {'id':
10751, 'name': 'Family'}]"
```

We can observe that the output is a stringified dictionary. In order for this feature to be usable, it is important that we convert this string into a native Python dictionary. Fortunately, Python gives us access to a function called `literal_eval` (available in the `ast` library) which does exactly that. `literal_eval` parses any string passed into it and converts it into its corresponding Python object:

```
#Import the literal_eval function from ast
from ast import literal_eval

#Define a stringified list and output its type
a = "[1,2,3]"
print(type(a))

#Apply literal_eval and output type
b = literal_eval(a)
print(type(b))
```

OUTPUT:
```
<class 'str'>
<class 'list'>
```

We now have all the tools required to convert the *genres* feature into the Python dictionary format.

Also, each dictionary represents a genre and has two keys: `id` and `name`. However, for this exercise (as well as all subsequent exercises), we only require the `name`. Therefore, we shall convert our list of dictionaries into a list of strings, where each string is a genre name:

```
#Convert all NaN into stringified empty lists
df['genres'] = df['genres'].fillna('[]')

#Apply literal_eval to convert to the list object
df['genres'] = df['genres'].apply(literal_eval)
```

```
#Convert list of dictionaries to a list of strings
df['genres'] = df['genres'].apply(lambda x: [i['name'] for i in x] if
isinstance(x, list) else [])

df.head()
```

Printing the head of the DataFrame should show you a new `genres` feature, which is a list of genre names. However, we're still not done yet. The last step is to `explode` the genres column. In other words, if a particular movie has multiple genres, we will create multiple copies of the movie, with each movie having one of the genres.

For example, if there is a movie called *Just Go With It* that has *romance* and *comedy* as its genres, we will `explode` this movie into two rows. One row will be *Just Go With It* as a *romance* movie. The other will be a *comedy* movie:

```
#Create a new feature by exploding genres
s = df.apply(lambda x:
pd.Series(x['genres']),axis=1).stack().reset_index(level=1, drop=True)

#Name the new feature as 'genre'
s.name = 'genre'

#Create a new dataframe gen_df which by dropping the old 'genres' feature
and adding the new 'genre'.
gen_df = df.drop('genres', axis=1).join(s)

#Print the head of the new gen_df
gen_df.head()
```

	title	runtime	vote_average	vote_count	year	genre
0	Toy Story	81.0	7.7	5415.0	1995	animation
0	Toy Story	81.0	7.7	5415.0	1995	comedy
0	Toy Story	81.0	7.7	5415.0	1995	family
1	Jumanji	104.0	6.9	2413.0	1995	adventure
1	Jumanji	104.0	6.9	2413.0	1995	fantasy

You should be able to see three *Toy Story* rows now; one each to represent *animation*, *family*, and *comedy*. This gen_df DataFrame is what we will use to build our knowledge-based recommender.

The build_chart function

We are finally in a position to write the function that will act as our recommender. We cannot use our computed values of *m* and *C* from earlier, as we will not be considering every movie just the ones that qualify. In other words, these are three main steps:

1. Get user input on their preferences
2. Extract all movies that match the conditions set by the user
3. Calculate the values of *m* and *C* for only these movies and proceed to build the chart as in the previous section

Therefore, the build_chart function will accept only two inputs: our gen_df DataFrame and the percentile used to calculate the value of *m*. By default, let's set this to 80%, or 0.8:

```
def build_chart(gen_df, percentile=0.8):
    #Ask for preferred genres
    print("Input preferred genre")
    genre = input()
    #Ask for lower limit of duration
    print("Input shortest duration")
    low_time = int(input())
    #Ask for upper limit of duration
    print("Input longest duration")
    high_time = int(input())
    #Ask for lower limit of timeline
    print("Input earliest year")
    low_year = int(input())
    #Ask for upper limit of timeline
    print("Input latest year")
    high_year = int(input())
    #Define a new movies variable to store the preferred movies. Copy the
contents of gen_df to movies
    movies = gen_df.copy()
    #Filter based on the condition
    movies = movies[(movies['genre'] == genre) &
                    (movies['runtime'] >= low_time) &
                    (movies['runtime'] <= high_time) &
                    (movies['year'] >= low_year) &
                    (movies['year'] <= high_year)]
    #Compute the values of C and m for the filtered movies
```

```
    C = movies['vote_average'].mean()
    m = movies['vote_count'].quantile(percentile)
    #Only consider movies that have higher than m votes. Save this in a new
dataframe q_movies
    q_movies = movies.copy().loc[movies['vote_count'] >= m]
    #Calculate score using the IMDB formula
    q_movies['score'] = q_movies.apply(lambda x:
(x['vote_count']/(x['vote_count']+m) * x['vote_average'])
                                    + (m/(m+x['vote_count']) * C)
                                    ,axis=1)

    #Sort movies in descending order of their scores
    q_movies = q_movies.sort_values('score', ascending=False)
    return q_movies
```

Time to put our model into action!

We want recommendations for animated movies between 30 minutes and 2 hours in length, and released anywhere between 1990 and 2005. Let's see the results:

```
In [114]: #Generate the chart for top animation movies and display top 5.
          build_chart(gen_df).head()

          Input preferred genre
          animation
          Input shortest duration
          30
          Input longest duration
          120
          Input earliest year
          1990
          Input latest year
          2005

Out[114]:
```

	title	runtime	vote_average	vote_count	year	genre	score
9698	Howl's Moving Castle	119.0	8.2	2049.0	2004	animation	7.994823
359	The Lion King	89.0	8.0	5520.0	1994	animation	7.926672
0	Toy Story	81.0	7.7	5415.0	1995	animation	7.637500
6232	Finding Nemo	100.0	7.6	6292.0	2003	animation	7.549423
546	The Nightmare Before Christmas	76.0	7.6	2135.0	1993	animation	7.460500

We can see that the movies that it outputs satisfy all the conditions we passed in as input. Since we applied IMDB's metric, we can also observe that our movies are very highly rated and popular at the same time. The top 5 also includes *The Lion King*, which is my favorite animated movie of all time! I, for one, would be very happy with the results of this list.

Summary

In this chapter, we built a simple recommender, which was a clone of the IMDB Top 250 chart. We then proceeded to build an improved knowledge-based recommender, which asked the user for their preferred genres, duration, and time. In the process of building these models, we also learned to perform some advanced data wrangling with the Pandas library.

In the next chapter, we will use more advanced features and techniques to build a content-based recommender. This model will be able to detect similar movies based on their plots and recommend movies by identifying similarities in genre, cast, crew, plot, and so on.

4
Building Content-Based Recommenders

In the previous chapter, we built an IMDB Top 250 clone (a type of simple recommender) and a knowledge-based recommender that suggested movies based on timeline, genre, and duration. However, these systems were extremely primitive. The simple recommender did not take into consideration an individual user's preferences. The knowledge-based recommender did take account of the user's preference for genres, timelines, and duration, but the model and its recommendations still remained very generic.

Imagine that Alice likes the movies *The Dark Knight, Iron Man*, and *Man of Steel.* It is pretty evident that Alice has a taste for superhero movies. However, our models from the previous chapter would not be able to capture this detail. The best it could do is suggest *action* movies (by making Alice input *action* as the preferred genre), which is a superset of superhero movies.

It is also possible that two movies have the same genre, timeline, and duration characteristics, but differ hugely in their audience. Consider *The Hangover* and *Forgetting Sarah Marshall,* for example. Both these movies were released in the first decade of the 21st century, both lasted around two hours, and both were comedies. However, the kind of audience that enjoyed these movies was very different.

An obvious fix to this problem is to ask the user for more metadata as input. For instance, if we introduced a *sub-genre* input, the user would be able to input values such as *superhero, black comedy*, and *romantic comedy*, and obtain more appropriate results, but this solution suffers heavily from the perspective of usability.

The first problem is that we do not possess data on *sub-genres*. Secondly, even if we did, our users are extremely unlikely to possess knowledge of their favorite movies' metadata. Finally, even if they did, they would certainly not have the patience to input it into a long form. Instead, what they would be more willing to do is tell you the movies they like/dislike and expect recommendations that match their tastes.

As we discussed in the first chapter, this is exactly what sites like Netflix do. When you sign up on Netflix for the first time, it doesn't have any information about your tastes for it to build a profile, leverage the power of its community, and give you recommendations with (a concept we'll explore in later chapters). Instead, what it does is ask you for a few movies you like and show you results that are most similar to those movies.

In this chapter, we are going to build two types of content-based recommender:

- **Plot description-based recommender:** This model compares the descriptions and taglines of different movies, and provides recommendations that have the most similar plot descriptions.
- **Metadata-based recommender:** This model takes a host of features, such as genres, keywords, cast, and crew, into consideration and provides recommendations that are the most similar with respect to the aforementioned features.

Technical requirements

You will be required to have Python installed on a system. Finally, to use the Git repository of this book, the user needs to install Git.

The code files of this chapter can be found on GitHub:
`https://github.com/PacktPublishing/Hands-On-Recommendation-Systems-with-Python`.

Check out the following video to see the code in action:

`http://bit.ly/2LOcac2`.

Exporting the clean DataFrame

In the previous chapter, we performed a series of data wrangling and cleaning processes on our metadata in order to convert it into a form that was more usable. To avoid having to perform these steps again, let's save this cleaned DataFrame into a CSV file. As always, doing this with pandas happens to be extremely easy.

In the knowledge recommender notebook from Chapter 4, enter the following code in the last cell:

```
#Convert the cleaned (non-exploded) dataframe df into a CSV file and save
it in the data folder
#Set parameter index to False as the index of the DataFrame has no inherent
meaning.
df.to_csv('../data/metadata_clean.csv', index=False)
```

Your `data` folder should now contain a new file, `metadata_clean.csv`.

Let's create a new folder, `Chapter 4`, and open a new Jupyter Notebook within this folder. Let's now import our new file into this Notebook:

```
import pandas as pd
import numpy as np

#Import data from the clean file
df = pd.read_csv('../data/metadata_clean.csv')

#Print the head of the cleaned DataFrame
df.head()
```

The cell should output a DataFrame that is already clean and in the desired form.

Document vectors

Essentially, the models we are building compute the pairwise similarity between bodies of text. But how do we numerically quantify the similarity between two bodies of text?

To put it another way, consider three movies: A, B, and C. How can we mathematically prove that the plot of A is more similar to the plot of B than to that of C (or vice versa)?

The first step toward answering these questions is to represent the bodies of text (henceforth referred to as documents) as mathematical quantities. This is done by representing these documents as vectors. In other words, every document is depicted as a series of n numbers, where each number represents a dimension and n is the size of the vocabulary of all the documents put together.

But what are the values of these vectors? The answer to that question depends on the *vectorizer* we are using to convert our documents into vectors. The two most popular vectorizers are CountVectorizer and TF-IDFVectorizer.

CountVectorizer

CountVectorizer is the simplest type of vectorizer and is best explained with the help of an example. Imagine that we have three documents, A, B, and C, which are as follows:

- **A**: The sun is a star.
- **B**: My love is like a red, red rose
- **C**: Mary had a little lamb

We now have to convert these documents into their vector forms using CountVectorizer. The first step is to compute the size of the vocabulary. The vocabulary is the number of unique words present across all documents. Therefore, the vocabulary for this set of three documents is as follows: the, sun, is, a, star, my, love, like, red, rose, mary, had, little, lamb. Consequently, the size of the vocabulary is 14.

It is common practice to not include extremely common words such as a, the, is, had, my, and so on (also known as stop words) in the vocabulary. Therefore, eliminating the stop words, our vocabulary, *V*, is as follows:

V: like, little, lamb, love, mary, red, rose, sun, star

The size of our vocabulary is now nine. Therefore, our documents will be represented as nine-dimensional vectors, and each dimension here will represent the number of times a particular word occurs in a document. In other words, the first dimension will represent the number of times like occurs, the second will represent the number of times little occurs, and so on.

Therefore, using the CountVectorizer approach, A, B, and C will now be represented as follows:

- **A**: (0, 0, 0, 0, 0, 0, 0, 1, 1)
- **B**: (1, 0, 0, 1, 0, 2, 1, 0, 0)
- **C**: (0, 1, 1, 0, 1, 0, 0, 0, 0)

TF-IDFVectorizer

Not all words in a document carry equal weight. We already observed this when we eliminated the stop words from our vocabulary altogether. But the words that were in the vocabulary were all given equal weighting.

But should this always be the case?

For example, consider a corpus of documents on dogs. Now, it is obvious that all these documents will frequently contain the word dog. Therefore, the appearance of the word *dog* isn't as important as another word that only appears in a few documents.

TF-IDFVectorizer (**Term Frequency-Inverse Document Frequency**)takes the aforementioned point into consideration and assigns weights to each word according to the following formula. For every word *i* in document *j*, the following applies:

$$w_{i,j} = tf_{i,j} \times \log(\tfrac{N}{df_i})$$

In this formula, the following is true:

- $w_{i,j}$ is the weight of word *i* in document *j*
- df_i is the number of documents that contain the term *i*
- *N* is the total number of documents

We won't go too much into the formula and the associated calculations. Just keep in mind that the weight of a word in a document is greater if it occurs more frequently in that document and is present in fewer documents. The weight $w_{i,j}$ takes values between 0 and 1:

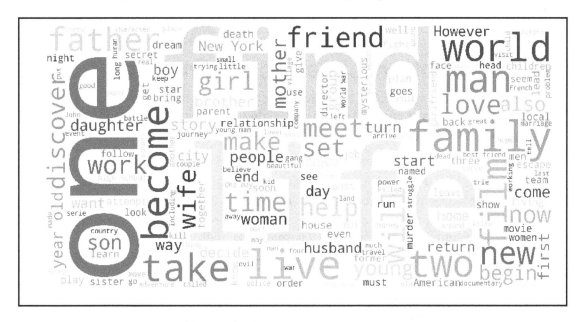

We will be using TF-IDFVectorizer because some words (pictured in the preceding word cloud) occur much more frequently in plot descriptions than others. It is therefore a good idea to assign weights to each word in a document according to the TF-IDF formula.

Another reason to use TF-IDF is that it speeds up the calculation of the cosine similarity score between a pair of documents. We will discuss this point in greater detail when we implement this in code.

The cosine similarity score

We will discuss similarity scores in detail in Chapter 5, *Getting Started with Data Mining Techniques*. Presently, we will make use of the *cosine similarity* metric to build our models. The cosine score is extremely robust and easy to calculate (especially when used in conjunction with TF-IDFVectorizer).

The cosine similarity score between two documents, x and y, is as follows:

$$cosine(x, y) = \frac{x.y^T}{||x||.||y||}$$

The cosine score can take any value between -1 and 1. The higher the cosine score, the more similar the documents are to each other. We now have a good theoretical base to proceed to build the content-based recommenders using Python.

Plot description-based recommender

Our plot description-based recommender will take in a movie title as an argument and output a list of movies that are most similar based on their plots. These are the steps we are going to perform in building this model:

1. Obtain the data required to build the model
2. Create TF-IDF vectors for the plot description (or overview) of every movie
3. Compute the pairwise cosine similarity score of every movie
4. Write the recommender function that takes in a movie title as an argument and outputs movies most similar to it based on the plot

Preparing the data

In its present form, the DataFrame, although clean, does not contain the features that are required to build the plot description-based recommender. Fortunately, these requisite features are available in the original metadata file.

All we have to do is import them and add them to our DataFrame:

```
#Import the original file
orig_df = pd.read_csv('../data/movies_metadata.csv', low_memory=False)

#Add the useful features into the cleaned dataframe
df['overview'], df['id'] = orig_df['overview'], orig_df['id']

df.head()
```

The DataFrame should now contain two new features: overview and id. We will use overview in building this model and id for building the next.

The overview feature consists of strings and, ideally, we should clean them up by removing all punctuation and converting all the words to lowercase. However, as we will see shortly, all this will be done for us automatically by scikit-learn, the library we're going to use heavily in building the models in this chapter.

Creating the TF-IDF matrix

The next step is to create a DataFrame where each row represents the TF-IDF vector of the overview feature of the corresponding movie in our main DataFrame. To do this, we will use the scikit-learn library, which gives us access to a TfidfVectorizer object to perform this process effortlessly:

```
#Import TfIdfVectorizer from the scikit-learn library
from sklearn.feature_extraction.text import TfidfVectorizer

#Define a TF-IDF Vectorizer Object. Remove all english stopwords
tfidf = TfidfVectorizer(stop_words='english')

#Replace NaN with an empty string
df['overview'] = df['overview'].fillna('')

#Construct the required TF-IDF matrix by applying the fit_transform method
on the overview feature
tfidf_matrix = tfidf.fit_transform(df['overview'])

#Output the shape of tfidf_matrix
tfidf_matrix.shape

OUTPUT:
(45466, 75827)
```

We see that the vectorizer has created a 75,827-dimensional vector for the overview of every movie.

Computing the cosine similarity score

The next step is to calculate the pairwise cosine similarity score of every movie. In other words, we are going to create a 45,466 × 45,466 matrix, where the cell in the ith row and j^{th} column represents the similarity score between movies i and j. We can easily see that this matrix is symmetric in nature and every element in the diagonal is 1, since it is the similarity score of the movie with itself.

Like TF-IDFVectorizer, `scikit-learn` also has functionality for computing the aforementioned similarity matrix. Calculating the cosine similarity is, however, a computationally expensive process. Fortunately, since our movie plots are represented as TF-IDF vectors, their magnitude is always 1. Hence, we do not need to calculate the denominator in the cosine similarity formula as it will always be 1. Our work is now reduced to computing the much simpler and computationally cheaper dot product (a functionality that is also provided by `scikit-learn`):

```
# Import linear_kernel to compute the dot product
from sklearn.metrics.pairwise import linear_kernel

# Compute the cosine similarity matrix
cosine_sim = linear_kernel(tfidf_matrix, tfidf_matrix)
```

Although we're computing the cheaper dot product, the process will still take a few minutes to complete. With the similarity scores of every movie with every other movie, we are now in a very good position to write our final recommender function.

Building the recommender function

The final step is to create our recommender function. However, before we do that, let's create a reverse mapping of movie titles and their respective indices. In other words, let's create a pandas series with the index as the movie title and the value as the corresponding index in the main DataFrame:

```
#Construct a reverse mapping of indices and movie titles, and drop
duplicate titles, if any
indices = pd.Series(df.index, index=df['title']).drop_duplicates()
```

We will perform the following steps in building the recommender function:

1. Declare the title of the movie as an argument.
2. Obtain the index of the movie from the `indices` reverse mapping.
3. Get the list of cosine similarity scores for that particular movie with all movies using `cosine_sim`. Convert this into a list of tuples where the first element is the position and the second is the similarity score.
4. Sort this list of tuples on the basis of the cosine similarity scores.
5. Get the top 10 elements of this list. Ignore the first element as it refers to the similarity score with itself (the movie most similar to a particular movie is obviously the movie itself).
6. Return the titles corresponding to the indices of the top 10 elements, excluding the first:

```
# Function that takes in movie title as input and gives recommendations
def content_recommender(title, cosine_sim=cosine_sim, df=df,
indices=indices):
    # Obtain the index of the movie that matches the title
    idx = indices[title]

    # Get the pairwsie similarity scores of all movies with that movie
    # And convert it into a list of tuples as described above
    sim_scores = list(enumerate(cosine_sim[idx]))

    # Sort the movies based on the cosine similarity scores
    sim_scores = sorted(sim_scores, key=lambda x: x[1], reverse=True)

    # Get the scores of the 10 most similar movies. Ignore the first movie.
    sim_scores = sim_scores[1:11]

    # Get the movie indices
    movie_indices = [i[0] for i in sim_scores]

    # Return the top 10 most similar movies
    return df['title'].iloc[movie_indices]
```

Congratulations! You've built your very first content-based recommender. Now it is time to see our recommender in action! Let's ask it for recommendations of movies similar to The Lion King:

```
#Get recommendations for The Lion King
content_recommender('The Lion King')
```

```
34682      How the Lion Cub and the Turtle Sang a Song
9353                               The Lion King 1½
9115                   The Lion King 2: Simba's Pride
42829                                           Prey
25654                                  Fearless Fagan
17041                                    African Cats
27933          Massaï, les guerriers de la pluie
6094                                        Born Free
37409                                      Sour Grape
3203                                 The Waiting Game
Name: title, dtype: object
```

We see that our recommender has suggested all of *The Lion King's* sequels in its top-10 list. We also notice that most of the movies in the list have to do with lions.

It goes without saying that a person who loves *The Lion King* is very likely to have a thing for Disney movies. They may also prefer to watch animated movies. Unfortunately, our plot description recommender isn't able to capture all this information.

Therefore, in the next section, we will build a recommender that uses more advanced metadata, such as genres, cast, crew, and keywords (or sub-genres). This recommender will be able to do a much better job of identifying an individual's taste for a particular director, actor, sub-genre, and so on.

Metadata-based recommender

We will largely follow the same steps as the plot description-based recommender to build our metadata-based model. The main difference, of course, is in the type of data we use to build the model.

Preparing the data

To build this model, we will be using the following metdata:

- The genre of the movie.
- The director of the movie. This person is part of the crew.
- The movie's three major stars. They are part of the cast.
- Sub-genres or keywords.

With the exception of genres, our DataFrames (both original and cleaned) do not contain the data that we require. Therefore, for this exercise, we will need to download two additional files: `credits.csv`, which contains information on the cast and crew of the movies, and `keywords.csv`, which contains information on the sub-genres.

 You can download the necessary files from the following URL: `https://www.kaggle.com/rounakbanik/the-movies-dataset/data`.

Place both files in your `data` folder. We need to perform a good amount of wrangling before the data is converted into a form that is usable. Let's begin!

The keywords and credits datasets

Let's start by loading our new data into the existing Jupyter Notebook:

```
# Load the keywords and credits files
cred_df = pd.read_csv('../data/credits.csv')
key_df = pd.read_csv('../data/keywords.csv')

#Print the head of the credit dataframe
cred_df.head()
```

	cast	crew	id
0	[{'cast_id': 14, 'character': 'Woody (voice)',...	[{'credit_id': '52fe4284c3a36847f8024f49', 'de...	862
1	[{'cast_id': 1, 'character': 'Alan Parrish', '...	[{'credit_id': '52fe44bfc3a36847f80a7cd1', 'de...	8844
2	[{'cast_id': 2, 'character': 'Max Goldman', 'c...	[{'credit_id': '52fe466a9251416c75077a89', 'de...	15602
3	[{'cast_id': 1, 'character': 'Savannah 'Vannah...	[{'credit_id': '52fe44779251416c91011acb', 'de...	31357
4	[{'cast_id': 1, 'character': 'George Banks', '...	[{'credit_id': '52fe44959251416c75039ed7', 'de...	11862

```
#Print the head of the keywords dataframe
key_df.head()
```

	id	keywords
0	862	[{'id': 931, 'name': 'jealousy'}, {'id': 4290,...
1	8844	[{'id': 10090, 'name': 'board game'}, {'id': 1...
2	15602	[{'id': 1495, 'name': 'fishing'}, {'id': 12392...
3	31357	[{'id': 818, 'name': 'based on novel'}, {'id':...
4	11862	[{'id': 1009, 'name': 'baby'}, {'id': 1599, 'n...

We can see that the cast, crew, and the keywords are in the familiar list of dictionaries form. Just like genres, we have to reduce them to a string or a list of strings.

Before we do this, however, we will join the three DataFrames so that all our features are in a single DataFrame. Joining pandas DataFrames is identical to joining tables in SQL. The key we're going to use to join the DataFrames is the id feature. However, in order to use this, we first need to explicitly convert is listed as an ID. This is clearly bad data. Therefore, we should fin
into an integer. We already know how to do this:

```
#Convert the IDs of df into int
df['id'] = df['id'].astype('int')
```

Running the preceding code results in a ValueError. On closer inspection, we see that *1997-08-20* is listed as an ID. This is clearly bad data. Therefore, we should find all the rows with bad IDs and remove them in order for the code execution to be successful:

```
# Function to convert all non-integer IDs to NaN
def clean_ids(x):
    try:
        return int(x)
    except:
        return np.nan

#Clean the ids of df
df['id'] = df['id'].apply(clean_ids)

#Filter all rows that have a null ID
df = df[df['id'].notnull()]
```

We are now in a good position to convert the IDs of all three DataFrames into integers and merge them into a single DataFrame:

```
# Convert IDs into integer
df['id'] = df['id'].astype('int')
key_df['id'] = key_df['id'].astype('int')
cred_df['id'] = cred_df['id'].astype('int')

# Merge keywords and credits into your main metadata dataframe
df = df.merge(cred_df, on='id')
df = df.merge(key_df, on='id')

#Display the head of the merged df
df.head()
```

	title	genres	runtime	vote_average	vote_count	year	overview	id	cast	crew	keywords
0	Toy Story	['animation', 'comedy', 'family']	81.0	7.7	5415.0	1995	Led by Woody, Andy's toys live happily in his ...	862	[{'cast_id': 14, 'character': 'Woody (voice)',...	[{'credit_id': '52fe4284c3a36847f8024f49', 'de...	[{'id': 931, 'name': 'jealousy'}, {'id': 4290,...
1	Jumanji	['adventure', 'fantasy', 'family']	104.0	6.9	2413.0	1995	When siblings Judy and Peter discover an encha...	8844	[{'cast_id': 1, 'character': 'Alan Parrish', '...	[{'credit_id': '52fe44bfc3a36847f80a7cd1', 'de...	[{'id': 10090, 'name': 'board game'}, {'id': 1...
2	Grumpier Old Men	['romance', 'comedy']	101.0	6.5	92.0	1995	A family wedding reignites the ancient feud be...	15602	[{'cast_id': 2, 'character': 'Max Goldman', 'c...	[{'credit_id': '52fe466a9251416c75077a89', 'de...	[{'id': 1495, 'name': 'fishing'}, {'id': 12392...
3	Waiting to Exhale	['comedy', 'drama', 'romance']	127.0	6.1	34.0	1995	Cheated on, mistreated and stepped on, the wom...	31357	[{'cast_id': 1, 'character': 'Savannah 'Vannah...	[{'credit_id': '52fe44779251416c91011acb', 'de...	[{'id': 818, 'name': 'based on novel'}, {'id':...
4	Father of the Bride Part II	['comedy']	106.0	5.7	173.0	1995	Just when George Banks has recovered from his ...	11862	[{'cast_id': 1, 'character': 'George Banks', '...	[{'credit_id': '52fe44959251416c75039ed7', 'de...	[{'id': 1009, 'name': 'baby'}, {'id': 1599, 'n...

Wrangling keywords, cast, and crew

Now that we have all the desired features in a single DataFrame, let's convert them into a form that is more usable. More specifically, these are the transformations we will be looking to perform:

- Convert `keywords` into a list of strings where each string is a keyword (similar to genres). We will include only the top three keywords. Therefore, this list can have a maximum of three elements.

- Convert `cast` into a list of strings where each string is a star. Like `keywords`, we will only include the top three stars in our cast.
- Convert `crew` into `director`. In other words, we will extract only the director of the movie and ignore all other crew members.

The first step is to convert these stringified objects into native Python objects:

```
# Convert the stringified objects into the native python objects
from ast import literal_eval

features = ['cast', 'crew', 'keywords', 'genres']
for feature in features:
    df[feature] = df[feature].apply(literal_eval)
```

Next, let's extract the director from our `crew` list. To do this, we will first examine the structure of the dictionary in the `crew` list:

```
#Print the first cast member of the first movie in df
df.iloc[0]['crew'][0]
```

OUTPUT:
```
{'credit_id': '52fe4284c3a36847f8024f49',
 'department': 'Directing',
 'gender': 2,
 'id': 7879,
 'job': 'Director',
 'name': 'John Lasseter',
 'profile_path': '/7EdqiNbr4FRjIhKHyPPdFfEEEFG.jpg'}
```

We see that this dictionary consists of `job` and `name` keys. Since we're only interested in the director, we will loop through all the crew members in a particular list and extract the `name` when the `job` is `Director`. Let's write a function that does this:

```
# Extract the director's name. If director is not listed, return NaN
def get_director(x):
    for crew_member in x:
        if crew_member['job'] == 'Director':
            return crew_member['name']
    return np.nan
```

Now that we have the `get_director` function, we can define the new `director` feature:

```
#Define the new director feature
df['director'] = df['crew'].apply(get_director)

#Print the directors of the first five movies
df['director'].head()

OUTPUT:
0  John Lasseter
1  Joe Johnston
2  Howard Deutch
3  Forest Whitaker
4  Charles Shyer
Name: director, dtype: object
```

Both `keywords` and `cast` are dictionary lists as well. And, in both cases, we need to extract the top three `name` attributes of each list. Therefore, we can write a single function to wrangle both these features. Also, just like `keywords` and `cast`, we will only consider the top three genres for every movie:

```
# Returns the list top 3 elements or entire list; whichever is more.
def generate_list(x):
    if isinstance(x, list):
        names = [ele['name'] for ele in x]
        #Check if more than 3 elements exist. If yes, return only first three.
        #If no, return entire list.
        if len(names) > 3:
            names = names[:3]
        return names

    #Return empty list in case of missing/malformed data
    return []
```

We will use this function to wrangle our `cast` and `keywords` features. We will also only consider the first three `genres` listed:

```
#Apply the generate_list function to cast and keywords
df['cast'] = df['cast'].apply(generate_list)
df['keywords'] = df['keywords'].apply(generate_list)

#Only consider a maximum of 3 genres
df['genres'] = df['genres'].apply(lambda x: x[:3])
```

Let's now take a look at a sample of our wrangled data:

```
# Print the new features of the first 5 movies along with title
df[['title', 'cast', 'director', 'keywords', 'genres']].head(3)
```

	title	cast	director	keywords	genres
0	Toy Story	[Tom Hanks, Tim Allen, Don Rickles]	John Lasseter	[jealousy, toy, boy]	[animation, comedy, family]
1	Jumanji	[Robin Williams, Jonathan Hyde, Kirsten Dunst]	Joe Johnston	[board game, disappearance, based on children'...	[adventure, fantasy, family]
2	Grumpier Old Men	[Walter Matthau, Jack Lemmon, Ann-Margret]	Howard Deutch	[fishing, best friend, duringcreditsstinger]	[romance, comedy]
3	Waiting to Exhale	[Whitney Houston, Angela Bassett, Loretta Devine]	Forest Whitaker	[based on novel, interracial relationship, sin...	[comedy, drama, romance]
4	Father of the Bride Part II	[Steve Martin, Diane Keaton, Martin Short]	Charles Shyer	[baby, midlife crisis, confidence]	[comedy]

In the subsequent steps, we are going to use a vectorizer to build document vectors. If two actors had the same first name (say, Ryan Reynolds and Ryan Gosling), the vectorizer will treat both Ryans as the same, although they are clearly different entities. This will impact the quality of the recommendations we receive. If a person likes Ryan Reynolds' movies, it doesn't imply that they like movies by all Ryans.

Therefore, the last step is to strip the spaces between keywords, and actor and director names, and convert them all into lowercase. Therefore, the two Ryans in the preceding example will become *ryangosling* and *ryanreynolds*, and our vectorizer will now be able to distinguish between them:

```
# Function to sanitize data to prevent ambiguity.
# Removes spaces and converts to lowercase
def sanitize(x):
    if isinstance(x, list):
        #Strip spaces and convert to lowercase
        return [str.lower(i.replace(" ", "")) for i in x]
    else:
        #Check if director exists. If not, return empty string
        if isinstance(x, str):
            return str.lower(x.replace(" ", ""))
        else:
            return ''

#Apply the generate_list function to cast, keywords, director and genres
for feature in ['cast', 'director', 'genres', 'keywords']:
    df[feature] = df[feature].apply(sanitize)
```

Creating the metadata soup

In the plot description-based recommender, we worked with a single *overview* feature, which was a body of text. Therefore, we were able to apply our vectorizer directly.

However, this is not the case with our metadata-based recommender. We have four features to work with, of which three are lists and one is a string. What we need to do is create a `soup` that contains the actors, director, keywords, and genres. This way, we can feed this soup into our vectorizer and perform similar follow-up steps to before:

```
#Function that creates a soup out of the desired metadata
def create_soup(x):
    return ' '.join(x['keywords']) + ' ' + ' '.join(x['cast']) + ' ' +
x['director'] + ' ' + ' '.join(x['genres'])
```

With this function in hand, we create the `soup` feature:

```
# Create the new soup feature
df['soup'] = df.apply(create_soup, axis=1)
```

Let's now take a look at one of the `soup` values. It should be a string containing words that represent genres, cast, and keywords:

```
#Display the soup of the first movie
df.iloc[0]['soup']
```

OUTPUT:
`'jealousy toy boy tomhanks timallen donrickles johnlasseter animation comedy family'`

With the `soup` created, we are now in a good position to create our document vectors, compute similarity scores, and build the metadata-based recommender function.

Generating the recommendations

The next steps are almost identical to the corresponding steps from the previous section.

Instead of using TF-IDFVectorizer, we will be using CountVectorizer. This is because using TF-IDFVectorizer will accord less weight to actors and directors who have acted and directed in a relatively larger number of movies.

This is not desirable, as we do not want to penalize artists for directing or appearing in more movies:

```
#Define a new CountVectorizer object and create vectors for the soup
count = CountVectorizer(stop_words='english')
count_matrix = count.fit_transform(df['soup'])
```

Unfortunately, using CountVectorizer means that we are forced to use the more computationally expensive `cosine_similarity` function to compute our scores:

```
#Import cosine_similarity function
from sklearn.metrics.pairwise import cosine_similarity

#Compute the cosine similarity score (equivalent to dot product for tf-idf
vectors)
cosine_sim2 = cosine_similarity(count_matrix, count_matrix)
```

Since we dropped a few movies with bad indices, we need to construct our reverse mapping again. Let's do that as the next step:

```
# Reset index of your df and construct reverse mapping again
df = df.reset_index()
indices2 = pd.Series(df.index, index=df['title'])
```

With the new reverse mapping constructed and the similarity scores computed, we can reuse the `content_recommender` function defined in the previous section by passing in `cosine_sim2` as an argument. Let's now try out our new model by asking recommendations for the same movie, The Lion King:

```
content_recommender('The Lion King', cosine_sim2, df, indices2)
```

```
29607                               Cheburashka
40904                 VeggieTales: Josh and the Big Wall
40913      VeggieTales: Minnesota Cuke and the Search for...
27768                           The Little Matchgirl
15209         Spiderman: The Ultimate Villain Showdown
16613                     Cirque du Soleil: Varekai
24654                         The Seventh Brother
29198                             Superstar Goofy
30244                                     My Love
31179         Pokémon: Arceus and the Jewel of Life
Name: title, dtype: object
```

The recommendations given in this case are vastly different to the ones that our plot description-based recommender gave. We see that it has been able to capture more information than just lions. Most of the movies in the list are animated and feature anthropomorphic characters.

Personally, I found the *Pokemon: Arceus and the Jewel of Life* recommendation especially interesting. Both this movie and *The Lion King* feature cartoon anthropomorphic characters who return after a few years to exact revenge on those who had wronged them.

Suggestions for improvements

The content-based recommenders we've built in this chapter are, of course, nowhere near the powerful models used in the industry. There is still plenty of scope for improvement. In this section, I will suggest a few ideas for upgrading the recommenders that you've already built:

- **Experiment with the number of keywords, genres, and cast**: In the model that we built, we considered at most three keywords, genres, and actors for our movies. This was, however, an arbitrary decision. It is a good idea to experiment with the number of these features in order to be considered for the metadata soup.

- **Come up with more well-defined sub-genres**: Our model only considered the first three keywords that appeared in the keywords list. There was, however, no justification for doing so. In fact, it is entirely possible that certain keywords appeared in only one movie (thus rendering them useless). A much more potent technique would be to define, as with the genres, a definite number of sub-genres and assign only these sub-genres to the movies.

- **Give more weight to the director**: Our model gave as much importance to the director as to the actors. However, you can argue that the character of a movie is determined more by the former. We can give more emphasis to the director by mentioning this individual multiple times in our soup instead of just once. Experiment with the number of repetitions of the director in the soup.

- **Consider other members of the crew**: The director isn't the only person that gives the movie its character. You can also consider adding other crew members, such as producers and screenwriters, to your soup.

- **Experiment with other metadata**: We only considered genres, keywords, and credits while building our metadata model. However, our dataset contains plenty of other features, such as production companies, countries, and languages. You may consider these data points, too, as they may be able to capture important information (such as if two movies are produced by *Pixar*).

- **Introduce a popularity filter**: It is entirely possible that two movies have the same genres and sub-genres, but differ wildly in quality and popularity. In such cases, you may want to introduce a popularity filter that considers the n most similar movies, computes a weighted rating, and displays the top five results. You have already learned how to do this in the previous chapter.

Summary

We have come a long way in this chapter. We first learned about document vectors and gained a brief introduction to the cosine similarity score. Next, we built a recommender that identified movies with similar plot descriptions. We then proceeded to build a more advanced model that leveraged the power of other metadata, such as genres, keywords, and credits. Finally, we discussed a few methods by which we could improve our existing system.

With this, we formally come to an end of our tour of content-based recommendation system. In the next chapters, we will cover what is arguably the most popular recommendation model in the industry today: collaborative filtering.

5
Getting Started with Data Mining Techniques

In 2003, Linden, Smith, and York of Amazon.com published a paper entitled Item-to-Item Collaborative Filtering, which explained how product recommendations at Amazon work. Since then, this class of algorithmg has gone on to dominate the industry standard for recommendations. Every website or app with a sizeable user base, be it Netflix, Amazon, or Facebook, makes use of some form of collaborative filters to suggest items (which may be movies, products, or friends):

As described in the first chapter, collaborative filters try to leverage the power of the community to give reliable, relevant, and sometime, even surprising recommendations. If Alice and Bob largely like the same movies (say The Lion King, Aladdin, and Toy Story) and Alice also likes Finding Nemo, it is extremely likely that Bob, who hasn't watched Finding Nemo, will like it too.

We will be building powerful collaborative filters in the next chapter. However, before we do that, it is important that we have a good grasp of the underlying techniques, principles, and algorithms that go into building collaborative filters.

Therefore, in this chapter, we will cover the following topics:

- **Similarity measures**: Given two items, how do we mathematically quantify how different or similar they are to each other? Similarity measures help us in answering this question.
  We have already made use of a similarity measure (the cosine score) while building our content recommendation engine. In this chapter, we will be looking at a few other popular similarity scores.
- **Dimensionality reduction**: When building collaborative filters, we are usually dealing with millions of users rating millions of items. In such cases, our user and item vectors are going to be of a dimension in the order of millions. To improve performance, speed up calculations, and avoid the curse of dimensionality, it is often a good idea to reduce the number of dimensions considerably, while retaining most of the information. This section of the chapter will describe techniques that do just that.
- **Supervised learning**: Supervised learning is a class of machine learning algorithm that makes use of label data to infer a mapping function that can then be used to predict the label (or class) of unlabeled data. We will be looking at some of the most popular supervised learning algorithms, such as support vector machines, logistic regression, decision trees, and ensembling.
- **Clustering**: Clustering is a type of unsupervised learning where the algorithm tries to divide all the data points into a certain number of clusters. Therefore, without the use of a label dataset, the clustering algorithm is able to assign classes to all the unlabel points. In this section, we will be looking at k-means clustering, a simple but powerful algorithm popularly used in collaborative filters.
- **Evaluation methods and metrics**: We will take a look at a few evaluation metrics that are used to gauge the performance of these algorithms. The metrics include accuracy, precision, and recall.

The topics covered in this chapter merit an entire textbook. Since this is a hands-on recommendation engine tutorial, we will not be delving too deeply into the functioning of most of the algorithms. Nor will we code them up from scratch. What we will do is gain an understanding of how and when they work, their advantages and disadvantages, and their easy-to-use implementations using the scikit-learn library.

Problem statement

Collaborative filtering algorithms try to solve the prediction problem (as described in the Chapter 1, *Getting Started with Recommender Systems*). In other words, we are given a matrix of i users and j items. The value in the ith row and the jth column (denoted by rij) denotes the rating given by user i to item j:

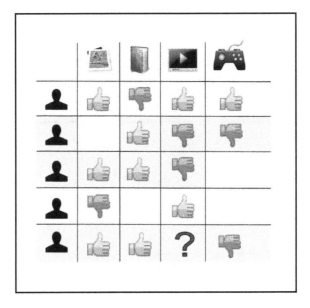

Matrix of i users and j items

Our job is to complete this matrix. In other words, we need to predict all the cells in the matrix that we have no data for. For example, in the preceding diagram, we are asked to predict whether user E will like the music player item. To accomplish this task, some ratings are available (such as User A liking the music player and video games) whereas others are not (for instance, we do not know whether Users C and D like video games).

Similarity measures

From the rating matrix in the previous section, we see that every user can be represented as a j-dimensional vector where the kth dimension denotes the rating given by that user to the kth item. For instance, let 1 denote a like, -1 denote a dislike, and 0 denote no rating. Therefore, user B can be represented as (0, 1, -1, -1). Similarly, every item can also be represented as an i-dimensional vector where the kth dimension denotes the rating given to that item by the kth user. The video games item is therefore represented as (1, -1, 0, 0, -1).

We have already computed a similarity score for like-dimensional vectors when we built our content-based recommendation engine. In this section, we will take a look at the other similarity measures and also revisit the cosine similarity score in the context of the other scores.

Euclidean distance

The Euclidean distance can be defined as the length of the line segment joining the two data points plotted on an *n*-dimensional Cartesian plane. For example, consider two points plotted in a 2D plane:

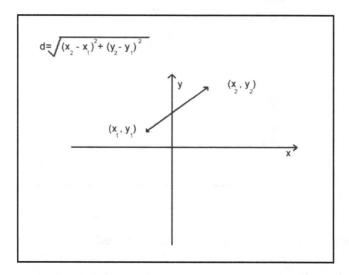

Euclidean distance

The distance, d, between the two points gives us the Euclidean distance and its formula in the 2D space is given in the preceding graph.

More generally, consider two *n*-dimensional points (or vectors):

- **v1**: (q1, q2,...., qn)
- **v2**: (r1, r2,...., rn)

Then, the Euclidean score is mathematically defined as:

$$d(v_1, v_2) = \sqrt{\sum_{i=1}^{n}(q_i - r_i)^2}$$

Euclidean scores can take any value between 0 and infinity. The lower the Euclidean score (or distance), the more similar the two vectors are to each other. Let's now define a simple function using NumPy, which allows us to compute the Euclidean distance between two *n*-dimensional vectors using the aforementioned formula:

```
#Function to compute Euclidean Distance.
def euclidean(v1, v2):
    #Convert 1-D Python lists to numpy vectors
    v1 = np.array(v1)
    v2 = np.array(v2)
    #Compute vector which is the element wise square of the difference
    diff = np.power(np.array(v1)- np.array(v2), 2)
    #Perform summation of the elements of the above vector
    sigma_val = np.sum(diff)
    #Compute square root and return final Euclidean score
    euclid_score = np.sqrt(sigma_val)
    return euclid_score
```

Next, let's define three users who have rated five different movies:

```
#Define 3 users with ratings for 5 movies
u1 = [5,1,2,4,5]
u2 = [1,5,4,2,1]
u3 = [5,2,2,4,4]
```

From the ratings, we can see that users 1 and 2 have extremely different tastes, whereas the tastes of users 1 and 3 are largely similar. Let's see whether the Euclidean distance metric is able to capture this:

```
euclidean(u1, u2)

OUTPUT:
7.4833147735478827
```

The Euclidean distance between users 1 and 2 comes out to be approximately 7.48:

```
euclidean(u1, u3)

OUTPUT:
1.4142135623730951
```

Users 1 and 3 have a much smaller Euclidean score between them than users 1 and 2. Therefore, in this case, the Euclidean distance was able to satisfactorily capture the relationships between our users.

Pearson correlation

Consider two users, Alice and Bob, who have rated the same five movies. Alice is extremely stingy with her ratings and never gives more than a 4 to any movie. On the other hand, Bob is more liberal and never gives anything below a 2 when rating movies. Let's define the matrices representing Alice and Bob and compute their Euclidean distance:

```
alice = [1,1,3,2,4]
bob = [2,2,4,3,5]

euclidean(alice, bob)

OUTPUT:
2.2360679774997898
```

We get a Euclidean distance of about 2.23. However, on closer inspection, we see that Bob always gives a rating that is one higher than Alice. Therefore, we can say that Alice and Bob's ratings are extremely correlated. In other words, if we know Alice's rating for a movie, we can compute Bob's rating for the same movie with high accuracy (in this case, by just adding 1).

Consider another user, Eve, who has the polar opposite tastes to Alice:

```
eve = [5,5,3,4,2]

euclidean(eve, alice)

OUTPUT:
6.324555320336759
```

We get a very high score of 6.32, which indicates that the two people are very dissimilar. If we used Euclidean distances, we would not be able to do much beyond this. However, on inspection, we see that the sum of Alice's and Eve's ratings for a movie always add up to 6. Therefore, although very different people, one's rating can be used to accurately predict the corresponding rating of the other. Mathematically speaking, we say Alice's and Eve's ratings are strongly negatively correlated.

Euclidean distances place emphasis on magnitude, and in the process, are not able to gauge the degree of similarity or dissimilarity well. This is where the Pearson correlation comes into the picture. The Pearson correlation is a score between -1 and 1, where -1 indicates total negative correlation (as in the case with Alice and Eve) and 1 indicates total positive correlation (as in the case with Alice and Bob), whereas 0 indicates that the two entities are in no way correlated with each other (or are independent of each other).

Mathematically, the Pearson correlation is defined as follows:

$$r = \frac{\sum_{i=1}^{n}(x_i - \bar{x})(y_i - \bar{y})}{\sqrt{\sum_{i=1}^{n}(x_i - \bar{x})^2}\sqrt{\sum_{i=1}^{n}(y_i - \bar{y})^2}}$$

Here, $\bar{i}$ denotes the mean of all the elements in vector i.

The SciPy package gives us access to a function that computes the Pearson Similarity Scores:

```
from scipy.stats import pearsonr

pearsonr(alice, bob)

OUTPUT:
(1.0, 0.0)

pearsonr(alice, eve)

OUTPUT:
(-1.0, 0.0)
```

The first element of our list output is the Pearson score. We see that Alice and Bob have the highest possible similarity score, whereas Alice and Eve have the lowest possible score. Can you guess the similarity score for Bob and Eve?

Cosine similarity

In the previous chapter, we mathematically defined the cosine similarity score and used it extensively while building our content-based recommenders:

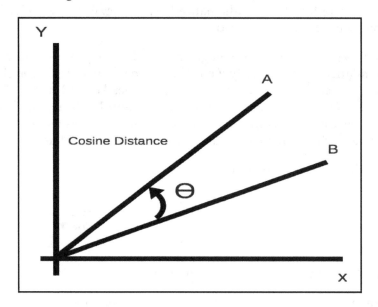

Mathematically, the Cosine similarity is defined as follows:

$$cosine(x, y) = \frac{x.y^T}{||x||.||y||}$$

The cosine similarity score computes the cosine of the angle between two vectors in an *n*-dimensional space. When the cosine score is 1 (or angle is 0), the vectors are exactly similar. On the other hand, a cosine score of -1 (or angle 180 degrees) denotes that the two vectors are exactly dissimilar to each other.

Now, consider two vectors, x and y, both with zero mean. We see that when this is the case, the Pearson correlation score is exactly the same as the cosine similarity Score. In other words, for centered vectors with zero mean, the Pearson correlation is the cosine similarity score.

Different similarity scores are appropriate in different scenarios. For cases where the magnitude is important, the Euclidean distance is an appropriate metric to use. However, as we saw in the case described in the Pearson correlation subsection, magnitude is not as important to us as correlation. Therefore, we will be using the Pearson and the cosine similarity scores when building our filters.

Clustering

One of the main ideas behind collaborative filtering is that if user A has the same opinion of a product as user B, then A is also more likely to have the same opinion as B on another product than that of a randomly chosen user.

Clustering is one of the most popular techniques used in collaborative-filtering algorithms. It is a type of unsupervised learning that groups data points into different classes in such a way that data points belonging to a particular class are more similar to each other than data points belonging to different classes:

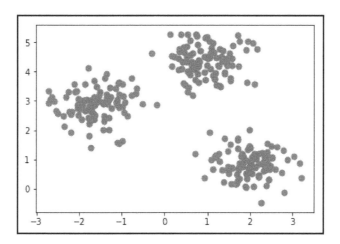

For example, imagine that all our users were plotted on a two-dimensional Cartesian plane, as shown in the preceding graph. The job of a clustering algorithm is to assign classes to every point on this plane. Just like the similarity measures, there is no one clustering algorithm to rule them all. Each algorithm has its specific use case and is suitable only in certain problems. In this section, we will be looking only at the k-means clustering algorithm, which will perform a satisfactory job is assigning classes to the collection of preceding points. We will also see a case where k-means will not prove to be suitable.

k-means clustering

The k-means algorithm is one of the simplest yet most popular machine learning algorithms. It takes in the data points and the number of clusters (k) as input.

Next, it randomly plots k different points on the plane (called centroids). After the k centroids are randomly plotted, the following two steps are repeatedly performed until there is no further change in the set of k centroids:

- Assignment of points to the centroids: Every data point is assigned to the centroid that is the closest to it. The collection of data points assigned to a particular centroid is called a cluster. Therefore, the assignment of points to k centroids results in the formation of k clusters.
- Reassignment of centroids: In the next step, the centroid of every cluster is recomputed to be the center of the cluster (or the average of all the points in the cluster). All the data points are then reassigned to the new centroids:

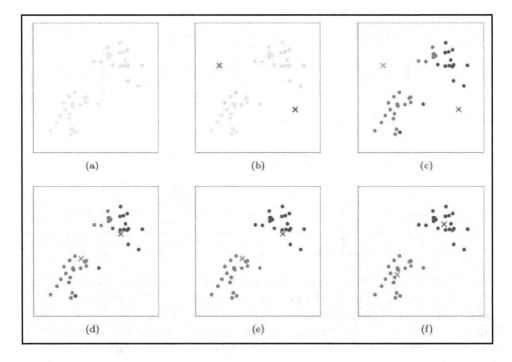

The preceding screenshot shows a visualization of the steps involved in a k-means clustering algorithm, with the number of assigned clusters as two.

Some sections in this chapter make use of the Matplotlib and Seaborn libraries for visualizations. You don't need to understand the plotting code written as part of this book, but if you're still interested, you can find the official matplotlib tutorial at `https://matplotlib.org/users/pyplot_tutorial.html` and the official seaborn tutorial at `https://seaborn.pydata.org/tutorial.html`.

We will not be implementing the k-means algorithm from scratch. Instead, we will use its implementation provided by scikit-learn. As a first step, let's access the data points as plotted in the beginning of this section:

```
#Import the function that enables us to plot clusters
from sklearn.datasets.samples_generator import make_blobs

#Get points such that they form 3 visually separable clusters
X, y = make_blobs(n_samples=300, centers=3,
                       cluster_std=0.50, random_state=0)



#Plot the points on a scatterplot
plt.scatter(X[:, 0], X[:, 1], s=50)
```

One of the most important steps while using the k-means algorithm is determining the number of clusters. In this case, it can be clearly seen from the plot (and the code) that we've plotted the points in such a way that they form three clearly separable clusters. Let's now apply the k-means algorithm via scikit-learn and assess its performance:

```
#Import the K-Means Class
from sklearn.cluster import KMeans

#Initializr the K-Means object. Set number of clusters to 3,
#centroid initilalization as 'random' and maximum iterations to 10
kmeans = KMeans(n_clusters=3, init='random', max_iter=10)

#Compute the K-Means clustering
kmeans.fit(X)

#Predict the classes for every point
y_pred = kmeans.predict(X)

#Plot the data points again but with different colors for different classes
plt.scatter(X[:, 0], X[:, 1], c=y_pred, s=50)

#Get the list of the final centroids
centroids = kmeans.cluster_centers_

#Plot the centroids onto the same scatterplot.
plt.scatter(centroids[:, 0], centroids[:, 1], c='black', s=100, marker='X')
```

We see that the algorithm proves to be extremely successful in identifying the three clusters. The three final centroids are also marked with an X on the plot:

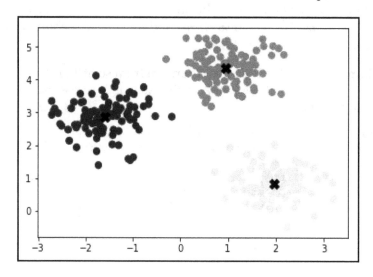

Choosing k

As stated in the previous subsection, choosing a good value of k is vital to the success of the k-means clustering algorithm. The number of clusters can be anywhere between 1 and the total number of data points (where each point is assigned to its own cluster).

Data in the real world is seldom of the type explored previously, where the points formed well defined, visually separable clusters on a two-dimensional plane. There are several methods available to determine a good value of K. In this section, we will explore the Elbow method of determining k.

The Elbow method computes the sum of squares for each value of k and chooses the elbow point of the sum-of-squares v/s K plot as the best value for k. The elbow point is defined as the value of k at which the sum-of-squares value for every subsequent k starts decreasing much more slowly.

The sum of squares value is defined as the sum of the distances of each data point to the centroid of the cluster to which it was assigned. Mathematically, it is expressed as follows:

$$SS = \sum_k \sum_{x_i \in C_k} (x_i - \mu_k)^2$$

Here, Ck is the kth cluster and uk is the corresponding centroid of Ck.

Fortunately for us, scikit-learn's implementation of k-means automatically computes the value of sum-of-squares when it is computing the clusters. Let's now visualize the Elbow plot for our data and determine the best value of K:

```
#List that will hold the sum of square values for different cluster sizes
ss = []

#We will compute SS for cluster sizes between 1 and 8.
for i in range(1,9):
    #Initialize the KMeans object and call the fit method to compute
clusters
    kmeans = KMeans(n_clusters=i, random_state=0, max_iter=10,
init='random').fit(X)
    #Append the value of SS for a particular iteration into the ss list
    ss.append(kmeans.inertia_)

#Plot the Elbow Plot of SS v/s K
sns.pointplot(x=[j for j in range(1,9)], y=ss)
```

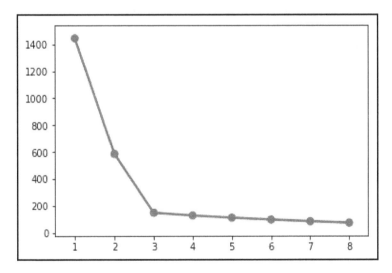

From the plot, it is clear that the Elbow is at K=3. From what we visualized earlier, we know that this is indeed the optimum number of clusters for this data.

Other clustering algorithms

The k-means algorithm, although very powerful, is not ideal for every use case.

To illustrate, let's construct a plot with two half moons. Like the preceding blobs, scikit-learn gives us a convenient function to plot half-moon clusters:

```
#Import the half moon function from scikit-learn
from sklearn.datasets import make_moons

#Get access to points using the make_moons function
X_m, y_m = make_moons(200, noise=.05, random_state=0)

#Plot the two half moon clusters
plt.scatter(X_m[:, 0], X_m[:, 1], s=50)
```

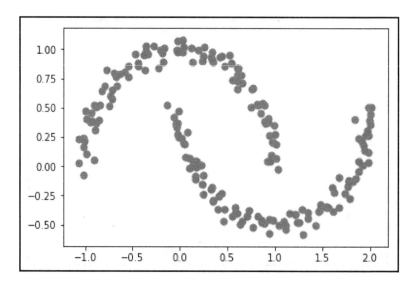

Will the k-means algorithm be able to figure out the two half moons correctly? Let's find out:

```
#Initialize K-Means Object with K=2 (for two half moons) and fit it to our
data
kmm = KMeans(n_clusters=2, init='random', max_iter=10)
kmm.fit(X_m)

#Predict the classes for the data points
y_m_pred = kmm.predict(X_m)

#Plot the colored clusters as identified by K-Means
plt.scatter(X_m[:, 0], X_m[:, 1], c=y_m_pred, s=50)
```

Let's now visualize what k-means thinks the two clusters that exist for this set of data points are:

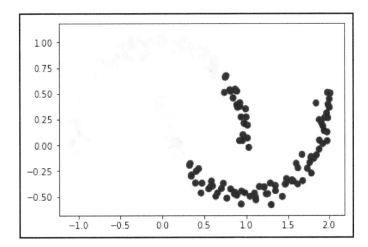

We see that the k-means algorithm doesn't do a very good job of identifying the correct clusters. For clusters such as these half moons, another algorithm, called spectral clustering, with nearest-neighbor, affinity performs much better.

We will not go into the workings of spectral clustering. Instead, we will use its scikit-learn implementation and assess its performance directly:

```
#Import Spectral Clustering from scikit-learn
from sklearn.cluster import SpectralClustering

#Define the Spectral Clustering Model
model = SpectralClustering(n_clusters=2, affinity='nearest_neighbors')

#Fit and predict the labels
y_m_sc = model.fit_predict(X_m)

#Plot the colored clusters as identified by Spectral Clustering
plt.scatter(X_m[:, 0], X_m[:, 1], c=y_m_sc, s=50)
```

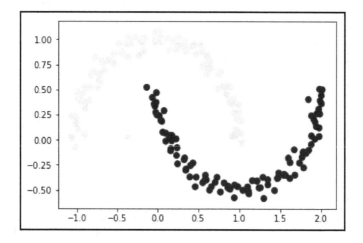

We see that spectral clustering does a very good job of identifying the half-moon clusters.

We have seen that different clustering algorithms are appropriate in different cases. The same applies to cases of collaborative filters. For instance, the surprise package, which we will visit in the next chapter, has an implementation of a collaborative filter that makes use of yet another clustering algorithm, called co-clustering. We will wrap up our discussion of clustering and move on to another important data mining technique: dimensionality reduction.

Dimensionality reduction

Most machine learning algorithms tend to perform poorly as the number of dimensions in the data increases. This phenomenon is often known as the curse of dimensionality. Therefore, it is a good idea to reduce the number of features available in the data, while retaining the maximum amount of information possible. There are two ways to achieve this:

- **Feature selection**: This method involves identifying the features that have the least predictive power and dropping them altogether. Therefore, feature selection involves identifying a subset of features that is most important for that particular use case. An important distinction of feature selection is that it maintains the original meaning of every retained feature. For example, let's say we have a housing dataset with price, area, and number of rooms as features. Now, if we were to drop the area feature, the remaining price and number of rooms features will still mean what they did originally.
- **Feature extraction**: Feature extraction takes in m-dimensional data and transforms it into an n-dimensional output space (usually where $m \gg n$), while retaining most of the information. However, in doing so, it creates new features that have no inherent meaning. For example, if we took the same housing dataset and used feature extraction to output it into a 2D space, the new features won't mean price, area, or number of rooms. They will be devoid of any meaning.

In this section, we will take a look at an important feature-extraction method: **Principal component analysis** (or **PCA**).

Principal component analysis

Principal component analysis is an unsupervised feature extraction algorithm that takes in m-dimensional input to create a set of n ($m \gg n$) linearly uncorrelated variables (called principal components) in such a way that the n dimensions lose as little variance (or information) as possible due to the loss of the (m-n) dimensions.

The linear transformation in PCA is done in such a way that the first principal component holds the maximum variance (or information). It does so by considering those variables that are highly correlated to each other. Every principal component has more variance than every succeeding component and is orthogonal to the preceding component.

Consider a three-dimensional space where two features are highly correlated to each other and relatively uncorrelated to the third:

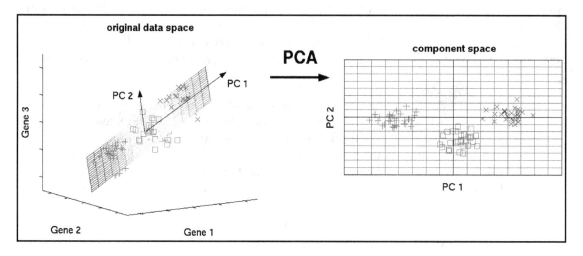

Let's say that we want to convert this into a two-dimensional space. To do this, PCA tries to identify the first principal component, which will hold the maximum possible variance. It does so by defining a new dimension using the two highly correlated variables. Now, it tries to define the next dimension in such a way that it holds the maximum variance, is orthogonal to the first principal component constructed, and also is uncorrelated to it. The two new dimensions (or principal components), PC 1 and PC 2, are shown in the preceding figure.

Understanding the PCA algorithm requires linear algebraic concepts that are beyond the scope of this book. Instead, we will use the black box implementation of PCA that `scikit-learn` gives us and consider a use case with the well-known Iris dataset.

The first step is to load the Iris dataset from the UCI machine learning repository into a pandas DataFrame:

```
# Load the Iris dataset into Pandas DataFrame
iris =
pd.read_csv("https://archive.ics.uci.edu/ml/machine-learning-databases/iris
/iris.data",
names=['sepal_length','sepal_width','petal_length','petal_width','class'])

#Display the head of the dataframe
iris.head()
```

	sepal_length	sepal_width	petal_length	petal_width	class
0	5.1	3.5	1.4	0.2	Iris-setosa
1	4.9	3.0	1.4	0.2	Iris-setosa
2	4.7	3.2	1.3	0.2	Iris-setosa
3	4.6	3.1	1.5	0.2	Iris-setosa
4	5.0	3.6	1.4	0.2	Iris-setosa

The PCA algorithm is extremely sensitive to scale. Therefore, we are going to scale all the features in such a way that they have a mean of 0 and a variance of 1:

```
#Import Standard Scaler from scikit-learn
from sklearn.preprocessing import StandardScaler

#Separate the features and the class
X = iris.drop('class', axis=1)
y = iris['class']

# Scale the features of X
X = pd.DataFrame(StandardScaler().fit_transform(X),
                 columns =
['sepal_length','sepal_width','petal_length','petal_width'])

X.head()
```

	sepal_length	sepal_width	petal_length	petal_width
0	-0.900681	1.032057	-1.341272	-1.312977
1	-1.143017	-0.124958	-1.341272	-1.312977
2	-1.385353	0.337848	-1.398138	-1.312977
3	-1.506521	0.106445	-1.284407	-1.312977
4	-1.021849	1.263460	-1.341272	-1.312977

We're now in a good place to apply the PCA algorithm. Let's transform our data into the two-dimensional space:

```
#Import PCA
from sklearn.decomposition import PCA

#Intialize a PCA object to transform into the 2D Space.
```

```
pca = PCA(n_components=2)

#Apply PCA
pca_iris = pca.fit_transform(X)
pca_iris = pd.DataFrame(data = pca_iris, columns = ['PC1', 'PC2'])

pca_iris.head()
```

	PC1	PC2
0	-2.264542	0.505704
1	-2.086426	-0.655405
2	-2.367950	-0.318477
3	-2.304197	-0.575368
4	-2.388777	0.674767

The `scikit-Learn`'s PCA implementation also gives us information about the ratio of variance contained by each principal component:

```
pca.explained_variance_ratio
```

OUTPUT:
array([0.72770452, 0.23030523])

We see that the first principal component holds about 72.8% of the information, whereas the second principal component holds about 23.3%. In total, 95.8% of the information is retained, whereas 4.2% of the information is lost in removing two dimensions.

Finally, let's visualize our data points by class in the new 2D plane:

```
#Concatenate the class variable
pca_iris = pd.concat([pca_iris, y], axis = 1)

#Display the scatterplot
sns.lmplot(x='PC1', y='PC2', data=pca_iris, hue='class', fit_reg=False)
```

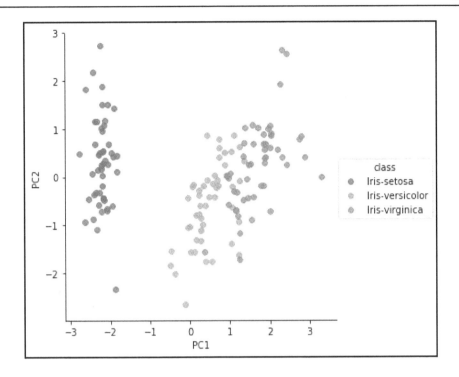

Other dimensionality reduction techniques

Linear-discriminant analysis

Like PCA, linear-discriminant analysis is a linear transformation method that aims to transform m-dimensional data into an n-dimensional output space.

However, unlike PCA, which tries to retain the maximum information, LDA aims to identify a set of n features that result in the maximum separation (or discrimination) of classes. Since LDA requires labeled data in order to determine its components, it is a type of supervised learning algorithm.

Let's now apply the LDA algorithm to the Iris dataset:

```
#Import LDA
from sklearn.discriminant_analysis import LinearDiscriminantAnalysis

#Define the LDA Object to have two components
lda = LinearDiscriminantAnalysis(n_components = 2)
```

```
#Apply LDA
lda_iris = lda.fit_transform(X, y)
lda_iris = pd.DataFrame(data = lda_iris, columns = ['C1', 'C2'])

#Concatenate the class variable
lda_iris = pd.concat([lda_iris, y], axis = 1)

#Display the scatterplot
sns.lmplot(x='C1', y='C2', data=lda_iris, hue='class', fit_reg=False)
```

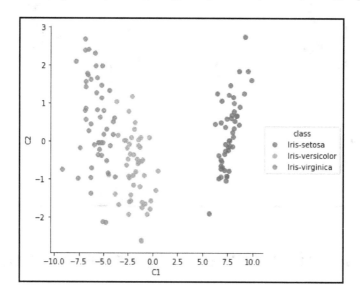

We see that the classes are much more separable than in PCA.

Singular value decomposition

Singular value decomposition, or SVD, is a type of matrix analysis technique that allows us to represent a high-dimensional matrix in a lower dimension. SVD achieves this by identifying and removing the less important parts of the matrix and producing an approximation in the desired number of dimensions.

The SVD approach to collaborative filtering was first proposed by Simon Funk and proved to be extremely popular and effective during the Netflix prize competition. Unfortunately, understanding SVD requires a grasp of linear algebraic topics that are beyond the scope of this book. However, we will use a black box implementation of the SVD collaborative filter as provided by the `surprise` package in the next chapter.

Supervised learning

Supervised learning is a class of machine learning algorithm that takes in a series of vectors and their corresponding output (a continuous value or a class) as input, and produces an inferred function that can be used to map new examples.

An important precondition for using supervised learning is the availability of labeled data. In other words, it is necessary that we have access to input for which we already know the correct output.

Supervised learning can be classified into two types: classification and regression. A classification problem has a discrete set of values as the target variable (for instance, a like and a dislike), whereas a regression problem has a continuous value as its target (for instance, an average rating between one and five).

Consider the rating matrix defined earlier. It is possible to treat (m-1) columns as the input and the mth column as the target variable. In this way, it should be possible to predict an unavailable value in the mth column by passing in the corresponding (m-1) dimensional vector.

Supervised learning is one of the most mature subfields of machine learning and, as a result, there are plenty of potent algorithms available for performing accurate predictions. In this section, we will look at some of the most popular algorithms used successfully in a variety of applications (including collaborative filters).

k-nearest neighbors

k-nearest neighbors (**k-NN**) is perhaps the simplest machine learning algorithm. In the case of classification, it assigns a class to a particular data point by a majority vote of its *k* nearest neighbors. In other words, the data point is assigned the class that is the most common among its k-nearest neighbors. In the case of regression, it computes the average value for the target variable based on its k-nearest neighbors.

Unlike most machine learning algorithms, k-NN is non-parametric and lazy in nature. The former means that k-NN does not make any underlying assumptions about the distribution of the data. In other words, the model structure is determined by the data. The latter means that k-NN undergoes virtually no training. It only computes the k-nearest neighbors of a particular point in the prediction phase. This also means that the k-NN model needs to have access to the training data at all times and cannot discard it during prediction like its sister algorithms.

Classification

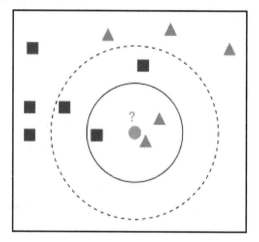

k-NN classification is best explained with the help of an example. Consider a dataset that has binary classes (represented as the blue squares and the red triangles). k-NN now plots this into *n*-dimensional space (in this case, two dimensions).

Let's say we want to predict the class of the green circle. Before the k-NN algorithm can make predictions, it needs to know the number of nearest neighbors that have to be taken into consideration (the value of *k*). *k* is usually odd (to avoid ties in the case of binary classification).

Consider the case where *k=3*.

k-NN computes the distance metric (usually the Euclidean distance) from the green circle to every other point in the training dataset and selects the three data points that are closest to it. In this case, these are the points contained in the solid inner circle.

The next step is to determine the majority class among the three points. There are two red triangles and one blue square. Therefore, the green circle is assigned the class of red triangle.

Now, consider the case where *k=5*.

In this case, the nearest neighbors are all the points contained within the dotted outer circle. This time around, we have two red triangles and three blue squares. Therefore, the green circle is assigned the class of blue square.

From the preceding case, it is clear that the value of *k* is extremely significant in determining the final class assigned to a data point. It is often a good practice to test different values of *k* and assess its performance with your cross-validation and test datasets.

Regression

k-NN regression works in almost the same way. Instead of classes, we compute the property values of the k-NN.

Imagine that we have a housing dataset and we're trying to predict the price of a house. The price of a particular house will therefore be determined by the average of the prices of the houses of its *k* nearest neighbors. As with classification, the final target value may differ depending on the value of *k*.

 For the rest of the algorithms in this section, we will go through only the classification process. However, just like k-NN, most algorithms require only very slight modifications to be suitable for use in a regression problem.

Support vector machines

The support vector machine is one of the most popular classification algorithms used in the industry. It takes in an *n*-dimensional dataset as input and constructs an *(n-1)* dimensional hyperplane in such a way that there is maximum separation of classes.

Consider the visualization of a binary dataset in the following screenshot:

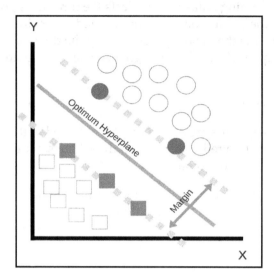

The preceding graph shows three possible hyperplanes (the straight lines) that separate the two classes. However, the solid line is the one with the maximum margin. In other words, it is the hyperplane that maximally separates the two classes. Also, it divides the entire plane into two regions. Any point below the hyperplane will be classified as a red square, and any point above will be classified as a blue circle.

The SVM model is only dependent on support vectors; these are the points that determine the maximum margin possible between the two classes. In the preceding graph, the filled squares and circles are the support vectors. The rest of the points do not have an effect on the workings of the SVM:

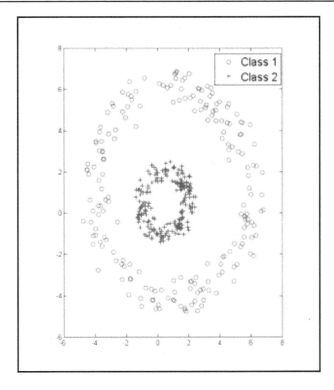

SVMs are also capable of separating classes that are not linearly separable (such as in the preceding figure). It does so with special tools, called radial kernel functions, that plot the points in a higher dimension and attempt to construct a maximum margin hyperplane there.

Decision trees

Decision trees are extremely fast and simple tree-based algorithms that branch out on features that result in the largest information gain. Decision trees, although not very accurate, are extremely interpretable.

We will not delve into the inner workings of the decision tree, but we will see it in action via a visualization:

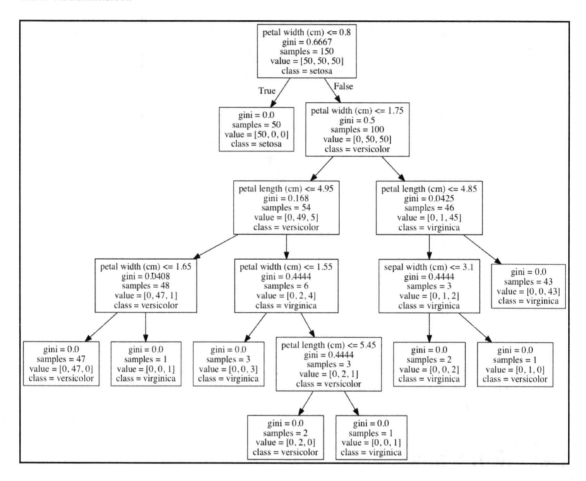

Let's say we want to classify the Iris dataset using a decision tree. A decision tree performing the classification is shown in the preceding diagram. We start at the top and go deeper into the tree until we reach a leaf node.

For example, if the petal width of a flower is less than 0.8 cm, we reach a leaf node and it gets classified as setosa. If not, it goes into the other branch and the process continues until a leaf node is reached.

Decision trees have an element of randomness in their workings and come up with different conditions in different iterations. As stated before, they are also not very accurate in their predictions. However, their randomness and fast execution make them extremely popular in ensemble models, which will be explained in the next section.

Ensembling

The main idea behind ensembling is that the predictive power of multiple algorithms is much greater than a single algorithm. Decision trees are the most common base algorithm used when building ensembling models.

Bagging and random forests

Bagging is short for bootstrap aggregating. Like most other ensemble methods, it averages over a large number of base classification models and averages their results to deliver its final prediction.

These are the steps involved in building a bagging model:

1. A certain percentage of the data points are sampled (say 10%). The Sampling is done with replacement. In other words, a particular data point can appear in multiple iterations.
2. A baseline classification model (typically a decision tree) is trained on this sampled data.
3. This process is repeated until n number of models are trained. The final prediction delivered by the bagging model is the average of all the predictions of all the base models.

An improvement on the bagging model is the random forest model. In addition to sampling data points, the random forest ensemble method also forces each baseline model to randomly select a subset of the features (usually a number equal to the square root of the total number of features):

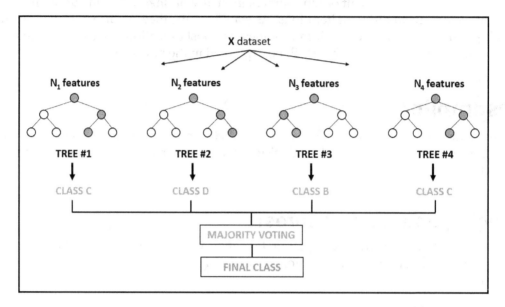

Selecting a subset of samples, as well as features, to build the baseline decision trees greatly enhances the randomness of each individual tree. This, in turn, increases the robustness of the random forest and allows it to perform extremely well with noisy data.

Additionally, building baseline models from a subset of features and analyzing their contribution to the final prediction also allows the random forest to determine the importance of each feature. It is therefore possible to perform feature-selection using random forests (recall that feature-selection is a type of dimensionality reduction).

Boosting

The bagging and the random forest models train baseline models that are completely independent of each other. Therefore, they do not learn from the mistakes that each learner has made. This is where boosting comes into play.

Like random forests, boosting models build a baseline model using a subset of samples and features. However, while building the next learners, the boosting model tries to rectify the mistakes that the previous learners made. Different boosting algorithms do this in different ways.

For example, the original boosting algorithm simply added 50% of the misclassified samples to the second learner, and all the samples that the first two learners disagree upon to build the third and final learner. This ensemble of three learners was then used to make predictions.

Boosting algorithms are extremely robust and routinely provide high performance. This makes them extremely popular in data science competitions and, as far as we are concerned, in building powerful collaborative filters.

The scikit-learn gives us access to implementations of all the algorithms described in this section. The usage of every algorithm is almost the same. As an illustration, let's apply gradient boosting to classify the Iris dataset:

```
#Divide the dataset into the feature dataframe and the target class series.
X, y = iris.drop('class', axis=1), iris['class']

#Split the data into training and test datasets.
#We will train on 75% of the data and assess our performance on 25% of the
data

#Import the splitting function
from sklearn.model_selection import train_test_split

#Split the data into training and test sets
X_train, X_test, y_train, y_test = train_test_split(X, y, test_size=0.25,
random_state=0)

#Import the Gradient Boosting Classifier
from sklearn.ensemble import GradientBoostingClassifier

#Apply Gradient Boosting to the training data
gbc = GradientBoostingClassifier()
gbc.fit(X_train, y_train)

#Compute the accuracy on the test set
gbc.score(X_test, y_test)

OUTPUT:
0.97368421052631582
```

We see that the classifier achieves a **97.3%** accuracy on the unseen test data. Like random forests, gradient boosting machines are able to gauge the predictive power of each feature. Let's plot the feature importances of the Iris dataset:

```
#Display a bar plot of feature importances
sns.barplot(x= ['sepal_length','sepal_width','petal_length','petal_width'],
y=gbc.feature_importances_)
```

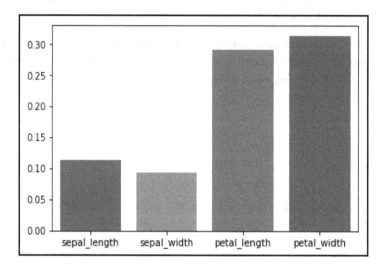

Evaluation metrics

In this section, we will take a look at a few metrics that will allow us to mathematically quantify the performance of our classifiers, regressors, and filters.

Accuracy

Accuracy is the most widely used metric to gauge the performance of a classification model. It is the ratio of the number of correct predictions to the total number of predictions made by the model:

$$Accuracy = \frac{Number\ of\ correct\ predictions}{Total\ number\ of\ predictions}$$

Root mean square error

The **Root Mean Square Error** (or **RMSE**) is a metric widely used to gauge the performance of regressors. Mathematically, it is represented as follows:

$$RMSE = \sqrt{\frac{1}{n} \sum (y_i - \hat{y}_i)^2}$$

Here, y_i is the ith real target value and $\hat{y}_i$ is the ith predicted target value.

Binary classification metrics

Sometimes, accuracy does not give us a good estimate of the performance of a model.

For instance, consider a binary class dataset where 99% of the data belongs to one class and only 1% of the data belongs to the other class. Now, if a classifier were to always predict the majority class for every data point, it would have 99% accuracy. But that wouldn't mean that the classifier is performing well.

For such cases, we make use of other metrics. To understand them, we first need to define a few terms:

- **True positive** (**TP**): True positive refers to all cases where the actual and the predicted classes are both positive
- **True negative** (**TN**): True negative refers to all cases where the actual and the predicted classes are both negative
- **False positive** (**FP**): These are all the cases where the actual class is negative but the predicted class is positive
- **False negative** (**FN**): These are all the cases where the actual class is positive but the predicted class is negative

To illustrate, consider a test that tries to determine whether a person has cancer. If the test predicts that a person does have cancer when in fact they don't, it is a false positive. On the other hand, if the test fails to detect cancer in a person actually suffering from it, it is a false negative.

Precision

The precision is the ratio of the number of positive cases that were correct to all the cases that were identified as positive. Mathematically, it looks like this:

$$Precision = \frac{TP}{TP + FP}$$

Recall

The recall is the ratio of the number of positive cases that were identified to the all positive cases present in the dataset:

$$Recall = \frac{TP}{TP + FN}$$

F1 score

The F1 score is a metric that conveys the balance between precision and recall. It is the harmonic mean of the precision and recall. An F1 score of 1 implies perfect precision and recall, whereas a score of 0 implies precision and recall are not possible:

$$F1 = 2.\frac{Precision \times Recall}{Precision + Recall}$$

Summary

In this chapter, we have covered a lot of topics that will help us to build powerful collaborative filters. We took a look at clustering, a form of unsupervised learning algorithm that could help us to segregate users into well defined clusters. Next, we went through a few dimensionality reduction techniques to overcome the curse of dimensionality and improve the performance of our learning algorithms.

The subsequent section dealt with supervised learning algorithms, and finally we ended the chapter with a brief overview of various evaluation metrics.

The topics covered in this chapter merit an entire book and we did not analyze the techniques in the depth usually required of machine learning engineers. However, what we have learned in this chapter should be sufficient to help us build and understand collaborative filters, which is one of the main objectives of this book. In case you're interested, a more detailed treatment of the topics presented in this chapter is available in an excellent book entitled *Python Machine Learning* by Sebastian Thrun.

6
Building Collaborative Filters

In the previous chapter, we mathematically defined the collaborative filtering problem and gained an understanding of various data mining techniques that we assumed would be useful in solving this problem.

The time has finally come for us to put our skills to the test. In the first section, we will construct a well-defined framework that will allow us to build and test our collaborative filtering models effortlessly. This framework will consist of the data, the evaluation metric, and a corresponding function to compute that metric for a given model.

Technical requirements

You will be required to have Python installed on a system. Finally, to use the Git repository of this book, the user needs to install Git.

The code files of this chapter can be found on GitHub:
`https://github.com/PacktPublishing/Hands-On-Recommendation-Systems-with-Python`.

Check out the following video to see the code in action:

`http://bit.ly/2mFmgRo`.

The framework

Just like the knowledge-based and content-based recommenders, we will build our collaborative filtering models in the context of movies. Since collaborative filtering demands data on user behavior, we will be using a different dataset known as MovieLens.

The MovieLens dataset

The MovieLens dataset is made publicly available by GroupLens Research, a computer science lab at the University of Minnesota. It is one of the most popular benchmark datasets used to test the potency of various collaborative filtering models and is usually available in most recommender libraries and packages:

MovieLens gives us user ratings on a variety of movies and is available in various sizes. The full version consists of more than 26,000,000 ratings applied to 45,000 movies by 270,000 users. However, for the sake of fast computation, we will be using the much smaller 100,000 dataset, which contains 100,000 ratings applied by 1,000 users to 1,700 movies.

Downloading the dataset

Without any further ado, let's go ahead and download the 100,000 dataset. The dataset available on the official GroupLens site does not provide us with user demographic information anymore. Therefore, we will use a legacy dataset made available on Kaggle by Prajit Datta.

 Download the MovieLens 100,000 dataset at `https://www.kaggle.com/ prajitdatta/movielens-100k-dataset/data`.

Unzip the folder and rename it `movielens`. Next, move this folder into the `data` folder within `RecoSys`. The MovieLens dataset should contain around 23 files. However, the only files we are interested in are `u.data`, `u.user`, and `u.item`. Let's explore these files in the next section.

Exploring the data

As mentioned in the previous section, we are only interested in three files in the `movielens` folder: `u.data`, `u.user`, and `u.item`. Although these files are not in CSV format, the code required to load them into a Pandas DataFrame is almost identical.

Let's start with `u.user`:

```
#Load the u.user file into a dataframe
u_cols = ['user_id', 'age', 'sex', 'occupation', 'zip_code']

users = pd.read_csv('../data/movielens/u.user', sep='|', names=u_cols,
  encoding='latin-1')

users.head()
```

Here is its output:

	user_id	age	sex	occupation	zip_code
0	1	24	M	technician	85711
1	2	53	F	other	94043
2	3	23	M	writer	32067
3	4	24	M	technician	43537
4	5	33	F	other	15213

We see that the `u.user` file contains demographic information about our users, such as their **age**, **sex**, **occupation**, and **zip_code**.

Next, let's take a look at the `u.item` file, which gives us information about the movies that have been rated by our users:

```
#Load the u.items file into a dataframe
i_cols = ['movie_id', 'title' ,'release date','video release date', 'IMDb
URL', 'unknown', 'Action', 'Adventure',
 'Animation', 'Children\'s', 'Comedy', 'Crime', 'Documentary', 'Drama',
'Fantasy',
 'Film-Noir', 'Horror', 'Musical', 'Mystery', 'Romance', 'Sci-Fi',
'Thriller', 'War', 'Western']

movies = pd.read_csv('../data/movielens/u.item', sep='|', names=i_cols,
encoding='latin-1')

movies.head()
```

Here is its output:

	movie id	movie title	release date	video release date	IMDb URL	unknown	Action	Adventure	Animation	Children's	...	Fantasy	Film-Noir	Horror	Musical	Myst
0	1	Toy Story (1995)	01-Jan-1995	NaN	http://us.imdb.com/M/title-exact?Toy%20Story%2...	0	0	0	1	1	...	0	0	0	0	
1	2	GoldenEye (1995)	01-Jan-1995	NaN	http://us.imdb.com/M/title-exact?GoldenEye%20(...	0	1	1	0	0	...	0	0	0	0	
2	3	Four Rooms (1995)	01-Jan-1995	NaN	http://us.imdb.com/M/title-exact?Four%20Rooms%...	0	0	0	0	0	...	0	0	0	0	
3	4	Get Shorty (1995)	01-Jan-1995	NaN	http://us.imdb.com/M/title-exact?Get%20Shorty%...	0	1	0	0	0	...	0	0	0	0	
4	5	Copycat (1995)	01-Jan-1995	NaN	http://us.imdb.com/M/title-exact?Copycat%20(1995)	0	0	0	0	0	...	0	0	0	0	

5 rows × 24 columns

We see that this file gives us information regarding the movie's title, **release date**, **IMDb URL**, and its genre(s). Since we are focused on building only collaborative filters in this chapter, we do not require any of this information, apart from the movie title and its corresponding ID:

```
#Remove all information except Movie ID and title
movies = movies[['movie_id', 'title']]
```

Lastly, let's import the `u.data` file into our notebook. This is arguably the most important file as it contains all the ratings that every user has given to a movie. It is from this file that we will construct our ratings matrix:

```
#Load the u.data file into a dataframe
r_cols = ['user_id', 'movie_id', 'rating', 'timestamp']

ratings = pd.read_csv('../data/movielens/u.data', sep='\t', names=r_cols,
 encoding='latin-1')

ratings.head()
```

Here is its output:

	user_id	movie_id	rating	timestamp
0	196	242	3	881250949
1	186	302	3	891717742
2	22	377	1	878887116
3	244	51	2	880606923
4	166	346	1	886397596

We see that every row in our new `ratings` DataFrame denotes a rating given by a user to a particular movie at a particular time. However, for the purposes of the exercises in this chapter, we are not really worried about the time at which the ratings were given. Therefore, we will just go ahead and drop it:

```
#Drop the timestamp column
ratings = ratings.drop('timestamp', axis=1)
```

Training and test data

The `ratings` DataFrame contains user ratings for movies that range from 1 to 5. Therefore, we can model this problem as an instance of supervised learning where we need to predict the rating, given a user and a movie. Although the ratings can take on only five discrete values, we will model this as a regression problem.

Consider a case where the true rating given by a user to a movie is 5. A classification model will not distinguish between the predicted ratings of 1 and 4. It will treat both as misclassified. However, a regression model will penalize the former more than the latter, which is the behavior we want.

As we saw in `Chapter 5`, *Getting Started with Data Mining Techniques*, one of the first steps towards building a supervised learning model is to construct the test and training sets. The model will learn using the training dataset and its potency will be judged using the testing dataset.

Let's now split our ratings dataset in such a way that 75% of a user's ratings is in the training dataset and 25% is in the testing dataset. We will do this using a slightly hacky way: we will assume that the `user_id` field is the target variable (or y) and that our `ratings` DataFrame consists of the predictor variables (or X). We will then pass these two variables into scikit-learn's `train_test_split` function and `stratify` it along y. This ensures that the proportion of each class is the same in both the training and testing datasets:

```
#Import the train_test_split function
from sklearn.model_selection import train_test_split

#Assign X as the original ratings dataframe and y as the user_id column of
ratings.
X = ratings.copy()
y = ratings['user_id']

#Split into training and test datasets, stratified along user_id
X_train, X_test, y_train, y_test = train_test_split(X, y, test_size = 0.25,
stratify=y, random_state=42)
```

Evaluation

We know from `Chapter 5`, *Getting Started with Data Mining Techniques* that the RMSE, or root mean squared error, is the most commonly used performance metric for regressors. We will be using the RMSE to assess our modeling performance too. `scikit-learn` already gives us an implementation of the mean squared error. So, all that we have to do is define a function that returns the square root of the value returned by `mean_squared_error`:

```
#Import the mean_squared_error function
from sklearn.metrics import mean_squared_error

#Function that computes the root mean squared error (or RMSE)
def rmse(y_true, y_pred):
    return np.sqrt(mean_squared_error(y_true, y_pred))
```

Next, let's define our baseline collaborative filter model. All our **collaborative filter** (or **CF**) models will take in a `user_id` and `movie_id` as input and output a floating point number between 1 and 5. We define our baseline model in such a way that it returns 3 regardless of `user_id` or `movie_id`:

```
#Define the baseline model to always return 3.
def baseline(user_id, movie_id):
    return 3.0
```

To test the potency of our model, we compute the RMSE obtained by that particular model for all user-movie pairs in the test dataset:

```
#Function to compute the RMSE score obtained on the testing set by a model
def score(cf_model):
    #Construct a list of user-movie tuples from the testing dataset
    id_pairs = zip(X_test['user_id'], X_test['movie_id'])
    #Predict the rating for every user-movie tuple
    y_pred = np.array([cf_model(user, movie) for (user, movie) in
id_pairs])
    #Extract the actual ratings given by the users in the test data
    y_true = np.array(X_test['rating'])
    #Return the final RMSE score
    return rmse(y_true, y_pred)
```

We're all set. Let's now compute the RMSE obtained by our baseline model:

```
score(baseline)
```

OUTPUT:
1.2470926188539486

We obtain a score of 1.247. For the models that we build in the subsequent sections, we will try to obtain an RMSE that is less than that obtained for the baseline.

User-based collaborative filtering

In Chapter 1, *Getting Started with Recommender Systems*, we learned what user-based collaborative filters do: they find users similar to a particular user and then recommend products that those users have liked to the first user.

In this section, we will implement this idea in code. We will build filters of increasing complexity and gauge their performance using the framework we constructed in the previous section.

To aid us in this process, let's first build a ratings matrix (described in Chapters 1, *Getting Started with Recommender Systems* and Chapter 5, *Getting Started with Data Mining Techniques*) where each row represents a user and each column represents a movie. Therefore, the value in the ith row and jth column will denote the rating given by user i to movie j. As usual, pandas gives us a very useful function, called pivot_table, to construct this matrix from our ratings DataFrame:

```
#Build the ratings matrix using pivot_table function
r_matrix = X_train.pivot_table(values='rating', index='user_id',
columns='movie_id')

r_matrix.head()
```

Here is its output:

movie_id user_id	1	2	3	4	5	6	7	8	9	10	...	1669	1670	1671	1673	1674	1675	1676	1679	1681	1682
1	5.0	3.0	4.0	3.0	3.0	5.0	4.0	1.0	5.0	3.0	...	NaN	NaN	NaN	NaN	NaN	NaN	NaN	NaN	NaN	NaN
2	NaN	NaN	NaN	NaN	NaN	NaN	NaN	NaN	NaN	2.0	...	NaN	NaN	NaN	NaN	NaN	NaN	NaN	NaN	NaN	NaN
3	NaN	NaN	NaN	NaN	NaN	NaN	NaN	NaN	NaN	NaN	...	NaN	NaN	NaN	NaN	NaN	NaN	NaN	NaN	NaN	NaN
4	NaN	NaN	NaN	NaN	NaN	NaN	NaN	NaN	NaN	NaN	...	NaN	NaN	NaN	NaN	NaN	NaN	NaN	NaN	NaN	NaN
5	NaN	3.0	NaN	NaN	NaN	NaN	NaN	NaN	NaN	NaN	...	NaN	NaN	NaN	NaN	NaN	NaN	NaN	NaN	NaN	NaN

5 rows × 1647 columns

We now have a new r_matrix DataFrame, where each row is a user and each column is a movie. Also, notice that most values in the DataFrame are unspecified. This gives us a picture of how sparse our matrix is.

Mean

Let's first build one of the simplest collaborative filters possible. This simply takes in `user_id` and `movie_id` and outputs the mean rating for the movie by all the users who have rated it. No distinction is made between the users. In other words, the rating of each user is assigned equal weight.

It is possible that some movies are available only in the test set and not the training set (and consequentially, not in our ratings matrix). In such cases, we will just default to a rating of 3.0, like the baseline model:

```
#User Based Collaborative Filter using Mean Ratings
def cf_user_mean(user_id, movie_id):
    #Check if movie_id exists in r_matrix
    if movie_id in r_matrix:
        #Compute the mean of all the ratings given to the movie
        mean_rating = r_matrix[movie_id].mean()
    else:
        #Default to a rating of 3.0 in the absence of any information
        mean_rating = 3.0
    return mean_rating

#Compute RMSE for the Mean model
score(cf_user_mean)
```

OUTPUT:
1.0234701463131335

We see that the score obtained for this model is lower and therefore better than the baseline.

Weighted mean

In the previous model, we assigned equal weights to all the users. However, it makes intuitive sense to give more preference to those users whose ratings are similar to the user in question than the other users whose ratings are not.

Therefore, let's alter our previous model by introducing a weight coefficient. This coefficient will be one of the similarity metrics that we computed in the previous chapter. Mathematically, it is represented as follows:

$$r_{u,m} = \frac{\sum_{u',u' \neq u} sim(u,u') \cdot r_{u',m}}{\sum_{u',u' \neq u} |sim(u,u')|}$$

In this formula, $r_{u,m}$ represents the rating given by user u to movie m.

For the sake of this exercise, we will use the cosine score as our similarity function (or sim). Recall how we constructed a movie cosine similarity matrix while building our content-based engine. We will be building a very similar cosine similarity matrix for our users in this section.

However, scikit-learn's `cosine_similarity` function does not work with NaN values. Therefore, we will convert all missing values to zero in order to compute our cosine similarity matrix:

```
#Create a dummy ratings matrix with all null values imputed to 0
r_matrix_dummy = r_matrix.copy().fillna(0)

# Import cosine_score
from sklearn.metrics.pairwise import cosine_similarity

#Compute the cosine similarity matrix using the dummy ratings matrix
cosine_sim = cosine_similarity(r_matrix_dummy, r_matrix_dummy)

#Convert into pandas dataframe
cosine_sim = pd.DataFrame(cosine_sim, index=r_matrix.index,
columns=r_matrix.index)

cosine_sim.head(10)
```

Here is its output:

user_id	1	2	3	4	5	6	7	8	9	10	...	934	935	936	937
user_id															
1	1.000000	0.099097	0.107680	0.034279	0.152789	0.086705	0.078864	0.068940	0.092399	0.098726	...	0.259636	0.289092	0.318824	0.149105
2	0.099097	1.000000	0.252131	0.026893	0.062539	0.039767	0.089474	0.078162	0.037670	0.031866	...	0.019031	0.065417	0.055373	0.086503
3	0.107680	0.252131	1.000000	0.000000	0.045543	0.078812	0.095354	0.059498	0.053879	0.074209	...	0.050703	0.056561	0.107294	0.098892
4	0.034279	0.026893	0.000000	1.000000	0.202843	0.299619	0.163724	0.038474	0.153021	0.290192	...	0.048524	0.048312	0.022202	0.091910
5	0.152789	0.062539	0.045543	0.202843	1.000000	0.375963	0.131795	0.110944	0.400758	0.181573	...	0.080312	0.162988	0.182856	0.114262
6	0.086705	0.039767	0.078812	0.299619	0.375963	1.000000	0.211282	0.107795	0.328923	0.253871	...	0.074170	0.094619	0.084235	0.115620
7	0.078864	0.089474	0.095354	0.163724	0.131795	0.211282	1.000000	0.037040	0.183375	0.126203	...	0.066843	0.058766	0.068759	0.087159
8	0.068940	0.078162	0.059498	0.038474	0.110944	0.107795	0.037040	1.000000	0.155435	0.032419	...	0.000000	0.101710	0.034568	0.045002
9	0.092399	0.037670	0.053879	0.153021	0.400758	0.328923	0.183375	0.155435	1.000000	0.164532	...	0.049310	0.153506	0.065471	0.060088
10	0.098726	0.031866	0.074209	0.290192	0.181573	0.253871	0.126203	0.032419	0.164532	1.000000	...	0.074822	0.092575	0.098653	0.136230

With the user cosine similarity matrix in hand, we are now in a position to efficiently calculate the weighted mean scores for this model. However, implementing this model in code is a little more nuanced than its simpler mean counterpart. This is because we need to only consider those cosine similarity scores that have a corresponding, non-null rating. In other words, we need to avoid all users that have not rated movie *m*:

```
#User Based Collaborative Filter using Weighted Mean Ratings
def cf_user_wmean(user_id, movie_id):
    #Check if movie_id exists in r_matrix
    if movie_id in r_matrix:
        #Get the similarity scores for the user in question with every
other user
        sim_scores = cosine_sim[user_id]

        #Get the user ratings for the movie in question
        m_ratings = r_matrix[movie_id]

        #Extract the indices containing NaN in the m_ratings series
        idx = m_ratings[m_ratings.isnull()].index

        #Drop the NaN values from the m_ratings Series
        m_ratings = m_ratings.dropna()

        #Drop the corresponding cosine scores from the sim_scores series
        sim_scores = sim_scores.drop(idx)
        #Compute the final weighted mean
        wmean_rating = np.dot(sim_scores, m_ratings)/ sim_scores.sum()
    else:
    #Default to a rating of 3.0 in the absence of any information
    wmean_rating = 3.0

    return wmean_rating


score(cf_user_wmean)
```

OUTPUT:
1.0174483808407588

Since we are dealing with positive ratings, the cosine similarity score will always be positive. Therefore, we do not need to explicitly add in a modulus function while computing the normalizing factor (the denominator of the equation that ensures the final rating is scaled back to between 1 and 5).

However, if you're working with a similarity metric that can be negative in this scenario (for instance, the Pearson correlation score), it is important that we factor in the modulus.

Running this code takes significantly more time than the previous model. However, we achieve a (very small) improvement in our RMSE score.

User demographics

Finally, let's take a look at filters that leverage user demographic information. The basic intuition behind these filter is that users of the same demographic tend to have similar tastes. Therefore, their effectiveness depends on the assumption that women, or teenagers, or people from the same area will share the same taste in movies.

Unlike the previous models, these filters do not take into account the ratings given by all users to a particular movie. Instead, they only look at those users that fit a certain demographic.

Let's now build a gender demographic filter. All this filter does is identify the gender of a user, compute the (weighted) mean rating of a movie by that particular gender, and return that as the predicted value.

Our ratings DataFrame does not contain the users' demographics. We will import that information from the users DataFrame by merging them into one (using pandas, as usual). Readers familiar with SQL can see that this is extremely similar to the JOIN functionality:

```
#Merge the original users dataframe with the training set
merged_df = pd.merge(X_train, users)

merged_df.head()
```

Here is its output:

	user_id	movie_id	rating	age	sex	occupation	zip_code
0	889	684	2	24	M	technician	78704
1	889	279	2	24	M	technician	78704
2	889	29	3	24	M	technician	78704
3	889	190	3	24	M	technician	78704
4	889	232	3	24	M	technician	78704

Next, we need to compute the `mean` rating of each movie by gender. Pandas makes this possible with the `groupby` method:

```
#Compute the mean rating of every movie by gender
gender_mean = merged_df[['movie_id', 'sex', 'rating']].groupby(['movie_id',
'sex'])            ['rating'].mean()
```

We are now in a position to define a function that identifies the gender of the user, extracts the average rating given to the movie in question by that particular gender, and return that value as output:

```
#Set the index of the users dataframe to the user_id
users = users.set_index('user_id')

#Gender Based Collaborative Filter using Mean Ratings
def cf_gender(user_id, movie_id):
    #Check if movie_id exists in r_matrix (or training set)
    if movie_id in r_matrix:
        #Identify the gender of the user
        gender = users.loc[user_id]['sex']
        #Check if the gender has rated the movie
        if gender in gender_mean[movie_id]:
            #Compute the mean rating given by that gender to the movie
            gender_rating = gender_mean[movie_id][gender]
        else:
            gender_rating = 3.0
    else:
        #Default to a rating of 3.0 in the absence of any information
        gender_rating = 3.0
    return gender_rating

score(cf_gender)
```

OUTPUT:
1.0330308800874282

We see that this model actually performs worse than the standard mean ratings collaborative filter. This indicates that a user's gender isn't the strongest indicator of their taste in movies.

Let's try building one more demographic filter, but this time using both gender and occupation:

```
#Compute the mean rating by gender and occupation
gen_occ_mean = merged_df[['sex', 'rating', 'movie_id',
'occupation']].pivot_table(
    values='rating', index='movie_id', columns=['occupation', 'sex'],
```

```
aggfunc='mean')

gen_occ_mean.head()
```

We see that the `pivot_table` method gives us the required DataFrame. However, this could have been done using `groupby` too. `pivot_table` is simply a more compact, easier-to-use interface for the `groupby` method:

```
#Gender and Occupation Based Collaborative Filter using Mean Ratings
def cf_gen_occ(user_id, movie_id):
    #Check if movie_id exists in gen_occ_mean
    if movie_id in gen_occ_mean.index:
        #Identify the user
        user = users.loc[user_id]
        #Identify the gender and occupation
        gender = user['sex']
        occ = user['occupation']
        #Check if the occupation has rated the movie
        if occ in gen_occ_mean.loc[movie_id]:
            #Check if the gender has rated the movie
            if gender in gen_occ_mean.loc[movie_id][occ]:
                #Extract the required rating
                rating = gen_occ_mean.loc[movie_id][occ][gender]
                #Default to 3.0 if the rating is null
                if np.isnan(rating):
                    rating = 3.0
                return rating
    #Return the default rating
    return 3.0

score(cf_gen_occ)
```

OUTPUT:
1.1391976012043645

We see that this model performs the worst out of all the filters we've built so far, beating only the baseline. This strongly suggests that tinkering with user demographic data may not be the best way to go forward with the data that we are currently using. However, you are encouraged to try different permutations and combinations of user demographics to see what performs best. You are also encouraged to try other techniques of improving the model, such as using a weighted mean for the `aggfunc` of the `pivot_table` and experimenting with different (perhaps more informed) default ratings.

Item-based collaborative filtering

Item-based collaborative filtering is essentially user-based collaborative filtering where the users now play the role that items played, and vice versa.

In item-based collaborative filtering, we compute the pairwise similarity of every item in the inventory. Then, given `user_id` and `movie_id`, we compute the weighted mean of the ratings given by the user to all the items they have rated. The basic idea behind this model is that a particular user is likely to rate two items that are similar to each other similarly.

Building an item-based collaborative filter is left as an exercise to the reader. The steps involved are exactly the same except now, as mentioned earlier, the movies and users have swapped places.

Model-based approaches

The collaborative filters we have built thus far are known as memory-based filters. This is because they only make use of similarity metrics to come up with their results.
They learn any parameters from the data or assign classes/clusters to the data. In other words, they do not make use of machine learning algorithms.

In this section, we will take a look at some filters that do. We spent an entire chapter looking at various supervised and unsupervised learning techniques. The time has finally come to see them in action and test their potency.

Clustering

In our weighted mean-based filter, we took every user into consideration when trying to predict the final rating. In contrast, our demographic-based filters only took users that fit a certain demographic into consideration. We saw that the demographic filters performed poorly compared to the weighted mean filter.

But does this necessarily imply that we need to take all users into consideration to achieve better results?

One of the major drawbacks of the demographic filters was that they were based on the assumption that people from a certain demographic think and rate alike. However, we can safely say that this is an overreached assumption. Not all men like action movies. Nor do all children like animated movies. Similarly, it is extremely far-fetched to assume that people from a particular area or occupation will have the same taste.

We need to come up with a way of grouping users with a much more powerful metric than demographics. From `Chapter 5`, *Getting Started with Data Mining Techniques*, we already know of one extremely powerful tool: `clustering`.

It is possible to use a clustering algorithm, such as k-means, to group users into a cluster and then take only the users from the same cluster into consideration when predicting ratings.

In this section, we will use k-means' sister algorithm, kNN, to build our clustering-based collaborative filter. In a nutshell, given an user, *u*, and a movie, *m*, these are the steps involved:

1. Find the k-nearest neighbors of *u* who have rated movie *m*
2. Output the average rating of the *k* users for the movie *m*

That's it. This extremely simply algorithm happens to be one of the most popularly used.

Just like kNN, we will not be implementing the kNN-based collaborative filter from scratch. Instead, we will use an extremely popular and robust library called `surprise`:

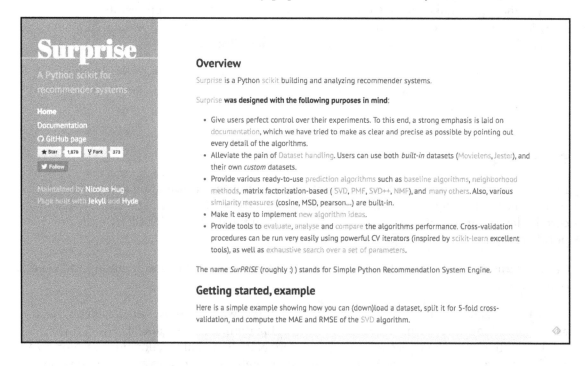

Surprise is a scikit (or scientific kit) for building recommender systems in Python. You can think of it as scikit-learn's recommender systems counterpart. According to its documentation, `surprise` stands for Simple Python Recommendation System Engine. Within a very short span of time, `surprise` has gone on to become one of the most popularly used recommender libraries. This is because it is extremely robust and easy to use. It gives us ready-to-use implementations of most of the popular collaborative filtering algorithms and also allows us to integrate an algorithm of our own into the framework.

To download `surprise`, like any other Python library, open up your Terminal and type the following command:

```
sudo pip3 install scikit-surprise
```

Let's now build and evaluate our kNN-based collaborative filter. Although *surprise* has the MovieLens datasets available within the library, we will still use the external data we have in order to get a feel for using the library with alien datasets:

```
#Import the required classes and methods from the surprise library
from surprise import Reader, Dataset, KNNBasic, evaluate

#Define a Reader object
#The Reader object helps in parsing the file or dataframe containing
ratings
reader = Reader()

#Create the dataset to be used for building the filter
data = Dataset.load_from_df(ratings, reader)

#Define the algorithm object; in this case kNN
knn = KNNBasic()

#Evaluate the performance in terms of RMSE
evaluate(knn, data, measures=['RMSE'])
```

Here is its output:

```
Evaluating RMSE of algorithm KNNBasic.

------------
Fold 1
Computing the msd similarity matrix...
Done computing similarity matrix.
RMSE: 0.9776
------------
Fold 2
Computing the msd similarity matrix...
Done computing similarity matrix.
RMSE: 0.9789
------------
Fold 3
Computing the msd similarity matrix...
Done computing similarity matrix.
RMSE: 0.9695
------------
Fold 4
Computing the msd similarity matrix...
Done computing similarity matrix.
RMSE: 0.9810
------------
Fold 5
Computing the msd similarity matrix...
Done computing similarity matrix.
RMSE: 0.9849
------------
------------
Mean RMSE: 0.9784
------------
------------
```

The output indicates that the filter is making use of a technique known as fivefold `cross-validation`. In a nutshell, this means that `surprise` divides the data into five equal parts. It then uses four parts as the training data and tests it on the fifth part. This is done five times, in such a way that every part plays the role of the test data once.

We see that the RMSE obtained by this model is **0.9784**. This is, by far, the best result we have achieved.

Let's now take a tour of some other model-based approaches to collaborative filtering and implement a few of them using the *surprise* library.

Supervised learning and dimensionality reduction

Consider our ratings matrix once again. It is of the $m \times n$ shape, where every row represents one of the m users and every column represents one of the n items.

Let's now remove one of the n columns (say n_j). We now have an $m \times (n-1)$ matrix. If we treat the $m \times (n-1)$ matrix as the predictor variables and n_j as the target variable, we can use supervised learning algorithms to train on the values available in n_j to predict values that are not. This can be repeated n times for every column to eventually complete our matrix.

One big problem is that most supervised learning algorithms do not work with missing data. In standard problems, it is common practice to impute the missing values with the mean or median of the column it belongs to.

However, our matrix suffers from heavy data sparsity. More than 99% of the data in the matrix is unavailable. Therefore, it is simply not possible to impute values (such as mean or median) without introducing a large bias.

One solution that may come to mind is to compress the predictor matrix in such a way that all the values are available. Unfortunately, dimensionality reduction techniques, such as SVD and PCA, also do not work in an environment with missing values.

While working toward a solution for the Netflix Problem, Simon Funk came up with a solution that could be used to reduce the $m \times (n-1)$ matrix into a lower-dimensional $m \times d$ matrix where $d \ll n$. He used standard dimensionality-reduction techniques (in his case, the SVD) but with slight tweaks. Explaining the technique is outside the scope of this book, but is presented in the Appendix for advanced readers. For the sake of this chapter, we will treat this technique as a black box that converts an $m \times n$ sparse matrix into an $m \times d$ dense matrix where $d \ll n$, and call it `SVD-like`.

Let's now turn our attention to perhaps the most famous recommendation algorithm of all time: singular-value decomposition.

Singular-value decomposition

In `Chapter 5`, *Getting Started with Data Mining Techniques*, we mentioned that the math behind singular-value decomposition is well outside the scope of this book. However, let's try to gain an understanding of how it works from a layman's perspective.

Recall from `Chapter 5`, *Getting Started with Data Mining Techniques,* that **PCA (Principal Component Analysis)** transforms an $m \times n$ matrix into n, m-dimensional vectors (called principal components) in such a way that each component is orthogonal to the next component. It also constructs these components in such a way that the first component holds the most variance (or information), followed by the second component, and so on.

Let's denote our ratings matrix as A. The transpose of this matrix would be A^T, which would be of the $n \times m$ shape and each row would represent a movie (instead of a user).

We can now use PCA to construct two new matrices, U and V, from A and A^T, respectively.

Singular-value decomposition allows us to compute U and V in one go from A:

In essence, singular-value decomposition is a matrix-factorization technique. It takes in an input, A, and outputs U and V such that:

$$A = U\Sigma V^T$$

Where Σ is a diagonal matrix. It is used for scaling purposes and, for the sake of this illustration, can be assumed to be merged with either U or V. Therefore, we now have:

$$A = UV^T$$

The U matrix, which is essentially composed of user principal components, is typically called the user-embedding matrix. Its counterpart, V, is called the movie-embedding matrix.

The classic version of SVD, like most other machine learning algorithms, does not work with sparse matrices. However, Simon Funk figured out a workaround for this problem, and his solution led to one of the most famous solutions in the world of recommender systems.

Funk's system took in the sparse ratings matrix, *A*, and constructed two dense user- and item-embedding matrices, *U* and *V* respectively. These dense matrices directly gave us the predictions for all the missing values in the original matrix, *A*.

Let's now implement the SVD filter using the `surprise` package:

```
#Import SVD
from surprise import SVD

#Define the SVD algorithm object
svd = SVD()

#Evaluate the performance in terms of RMSE
evaluate(svd, data, measures=['RMSE'])
```

Here is its output:

```
Evaluating RMSE of algorithm SVD.

------------
Fold 1
RMSE: 0.9371
------------
Fold 2
RMSE: 0.9417
------------
Fold 3
RMSE: 0.9289
------------
Fold 4
RMSE: 0.9379
------------
Fold 5
RMSE: 0.9379
------------
------------
Mean RMSE: 0.9367
------------
------------
```

The SVD filter outperforms all other filters, with an RMSE score of **0.9367**.

Summary

This brings us to the end of our discussion on collaborative filters. In this chapter, we built various kinds of user-based collaborative filters and, by extension, learned to build item-based collaborative filters as well.

We then shifted our focus to model-based approaches that rely on machine learning algorithms to churn out predictions. We were introduced to the *surprise* library and used it to implement a clustering model based on kNN. We then took a look at an approach to using supervised learning algorithms to predict the missing values in the ratings matrix. Finally, we gained a layman's understanding of the singular-value decomposition algorithm and implemented it using `surprise`.

All the recommenders we've built so far reside only inside our Jupyter Notebooks. In the next chapter, we will learn how to deploy our models to the web, where they can be used by anyone on the internet.

7
Hybrid Recommenders

In this final chapter, we will discuss recommender systems in the context of practicality and industrial use. Until now, we have learned about various types of recommender, including knowledge, content, and collaborative filtering-based engines. However, when used in practice, each recommender usually suffers from one shortcoming or another.

We've discussed these shortcomings in the very first chapter (for instance, the novelty problem of content-based engines and the cold start problem of collaborative filters). We also briefly introduced the concept of the hybrid recommender: a robust system that combines various models to combat the disadvantage of one model with the advantage of another. In this chapter, we will build a simple hybrid recommender that combines the content and the collaborative filters that we've built thus far.

Technical requirements

You will be required to have Python installed on a system. Finally, to use the Git repository of this book, the user needs to install Git.

The code files of this chapter can be found on GitHub:
https://github.com/PacktPublishing/Hands-On-Recommendation-Systems-with-Python.

Check out the following video to see the code in action:

http://bit.ly/2uOHwcd.

Introduction

As already mentioned a couple of times, hybrid recommenders are extremely powerful, robust systems that combine various simpler models to give us predictions. There is no single way in which a hybrid model could do this; some hybrids predict using content and collaborative filtering techniques separately to produce results. Some others introduce content-based techniques into collaborative filters and vice versa.

Netflix is a very good example of a hybrid recommender. Netflix employs content-based techniques when it shows you similar movies to a movie you're watching (the **MORE LIKE THIS** section), as shown in the following screenshot:

Here, we can see that while watching *Ratatouille,* Netflix recommends movies to me that are very similar to *Ratatouille.* All the top five recommended movies are all animated and produced by Disney Pixar.

However, animated movies are not the only genre I watch on Netflix. I also like watching drama and comedy. Netflix has a separate row of recommendations for me entitled **Top Picks for Rounak**, where it uses collaborative filtering to identify users similar to me and recommend movies that they have liked, but that I haven't watched:

In this way, Netflix employs both content- and collaborative-based techniques separately to produce results that are extremely satisfactory.

Case study – Building a hybrid model

In this section, let's build a content-based model that incorporates some collaborative filtering techniques into it.

Imagine that you have built a website like Netflix. Every time a user watches a movie, you want to display a list of recommendations in the side pane (like YouTube). At first glance, a content-based recommender seems appropriate for this task. This is because, if the person is currently watching something they find interesting, they will be more inclined to watch something similar to it.

Let's say our user is watching *The Dark Knight*. Since this is a Batman movie, our content-based recommender is likely to recommend other Batman (or superhero) movies regardless of quality. This may not always lead to the best recommendations. For instance, most people who like *The Dark Knight* do not rate *Batman and Robin* very highly, although they feature the same lead character. Therefore, we will introduce a collaborative filter here that predicts the ratings of the movies recommended by our content-based model and return the top few movies with the highest predictions.

In other words, the workflow of our hybrid model will be as follows:

1. Take in a movie title and user as input
2. Use a content-based model to compute the 25 most similar movies
3. Compute the predicted ratings that the user might give these 25 movies using a collaborative filter
4. Return the top 10 movies with the highest predicted rating

We will be using different datasets for this task. Go ahead and download the datasets from the following links.

Download the following datasets from Kaggle and Google Drive:

- `ratings_small.csv`: https://www.kaggle.com/rounakbanik/the-movies-dataset/downloads/ratings_small.csv/7.
- `movie_ids.csv`: https://drive.google.com/drive/folders/1H9pnfVTzP46s7VwOTcC5ZY_VahRTr5Zv?usp=sharing.

The `ratings_small.csv` file contains 100,000 ratings for 9,000 movies from 700 users. We use this file since it contains ratings for more recent movies (the dataset we used for collaborative filtering only contained movies released before 1998).

The `links_small.csv` file contains the movie IDs of all the movies rated in the `ratings_small.csv` file and their corresponding titles. We can use these IDs to extract relevant metadata from the `movies_metadata.csv` file.

With these files in hand, let's proceed to build our model. The first step is to compute the `cosine_sim` matrix for our movies. In addition, we also need to map every movie to the indices in the `cosine_sim` matrix. We've already learned how to do this in Chapter 3, *Building an IMDB Top 250 Clone with Pandas*. Computing this matrix and the mapping, therefore, is left as an exercise for the reader.

You can download my `cosine_sim` and `cosine_sim_map` files from the following link:
https://drive.google.com/drive/folders/1H9pnfVTzP46s7VwOTcC5ZY_VahRTr5Zv?usp=sharing. However, be aware that the `cosine_sim` file is over 1 GB in size, and therefore might take some time to download.

Next, let's use the `ratings.csv` file to build a collaborative filtering model. We will use the SVD model from the last chapter for this purpose:

```
#Build the SVD based Collaborative filter
from surprise import SVD, Reader, Dataset

reader = Reader()
ratings = pd.read_csv('../data/ratings_small.csv')
data = Dataset.load_from_df(ratings[['userId', 'movieId', 'rating']],
reader)
data.split(n_folds=5)
svd = SVD()
trainset = data.build_full_trainset()
svd.train(trainset)
```

Next, let's load the `movie_ids.csv` file into a DataFrame and construct two mappings: one that returns the movie title for a given movie ID, and the other vice versa:

```
#Build title to ID and ID to title mappings
id_map = pd.read_csv('../data/movie_ids.csv')
id_to_title = id_map.set_index('id')
title_to_id = id_map.set_index('title')
```

Now, let's import the metadata for our movies so that our recommender can display useful information, such as the IMDB rating and the year of release. This information can be extracted from the main `movies_metadata.csv` file, and is again left as an exercise for the reader.

> You can download the required metadata file from the following link:
> `https://drive.google.com/drive/folders/1H9pnfVTzP46s7VwOTcC5ZY_VahRTr5Zv?usp=sharing`

We're finally in a position to build the hybrid recommender function according to the workflow described previously:

```
def hybrid(userId, title):
    #Extract the cosine_sim index of the movie
    idx = cosine_sim_map[title]
    #Extract the TMDB ID of the movie
    tmdbId = title_to_id.loc[title]['id']
    #Extract the movie ID internally assigned by the dataset
    movie_id = title_to_id.loc[title]['movieId']
    #Extract the similarity scores and their corresponding index for every
movie from the cosine_sim matrix
    sim_scores = list(enumerate(cosine_sim[str(int(idx))]))
    #Sort the (index, score) tuples in decreasing order of similarity
scores
    sim_scores = sorted(sim_scores, key=lambda x: x[1], reverse=True)
    #Select the top 25 tuples, excluding the first
    #(as it is the similarity score of the movie with itself)
    sim_scores = sim_scores[1:26]
    #Store the cosine_sim indices of the top 25 movies in a list
    movie_indices = [i[0] for i in sim_scores]

    #Extract the metadata of the aforementioned movies
    movies = smd.iloc[movie_indices][['title', 'vote_count',
'vote_average', 'year', 'id']]
    #Compute the predicted ratings using the SVD filter
    movies['est'] = movies['id'].apply(lambda x: svd.predict(userId,
id_to_title.loc[x]['movieId']).est)
    #Sort the movies in decreasing order of predicted rating
```

```
movies = movies.sort_values('est', ascending=False)
#Return the top 10 movies as recommendations
return movies.head(10)
```

Let's put our hybrid model to the test. Let's imagine that users with the IDs 1 and 2 are both watching the movie *Avatar:*

```
hybrid(1, 'Avatar')
```

	title	vote_count	vote_average	year	id	est
1011	The Terminator	4208.0	7.4	1984	218	3.140748
974	Aliens	3282.0	7.7	1986	679	3.126947
8401	Star Trek Into Darkness	4479.0	7.4	2013	54138	3.079551
7705	Alice in Wonderland	8.0	5.4	1933	25694	3.054995
3060	Sinbad and the Eye of the Tiger	39.0	6.3	1977	11940	3.028386
8658	X-Men: Days of Future Past	6155.0	7.5	2014	127585	2.997411
2014	Fantastic Planet	140.0	7.6	1973	16306	2.957614
522	Terminator 2: Judgment Day	4274.0	7.7	1991	280	2.914548
1621	Darby O'Gill and the Little People	35.0	6.7	1959	18887	2.844940
1668	Return from Witch Mountain	38.0	5.6	1978	14822	2.804012

```
hybrid(2, 'Avatar')
```

	title	vote_count	vote_average	year	id	est
522	Terminator 2: Judgment Day	4274.0	7.7	1991	280	3.943639
2834	Predator	2129.0	7.3	1987	106	3.866272
8401	Star Trek Into Darkness	4479.0	7.4	2013	54138	3.858491
1011	The Terminator	4208.0	7.4	1984	218	3.856029
7705	Alice in Wonderland	8.0	5.4	1933	25694	3.701565
922	The Abyss	822.0	7.1	1989	2756	3.676465
974	Aliens	3282.0	7.7	1986	679	3.672303
1621	Darby O'Gill and the Little People	35.0	6.7	1959	18887	3.628234
1668	Return from Witch Mountain	38.0	5.6	1978	14822	3.614118
2014	Fantastic Planet	140.0	7.6	1973	16306	3.602051

We can see that although both users are currently watching *Avatar*, the recommendations differ in the content as well as the order. This is influenced by the collaborative filter. However, all the movies listed are similar to *Avatar*. This is because of the content-based filtering carried out by the model.

Following this section may have been a little hard, especially if you do not recall the material covered in `Chapter 3`, *Building an IMDB Top 250 Clone with Pandas*. I strongly recommend going back and rereading the chapter if something doesn't make sense. For reference, the entire code for this model can be found in the `Chapter7` folder of the `RecoSys` repository.

Summary

With this, we come to the end of this chapter, as well as the main part of the book. In this book, we learned the following:

- We were introduced to the world of recommender systems. We defined the recommendation problem mathematically and discussed the various types of recommendation engines that exist, as well as their advantages and disadvantages.
- We then learned to perform data wrangling with the pandas library and familiarized ourselves with two of pandas, most powerful data structures: the series and the DataFrame.
- With our newly found data wrangling techniques, we proceeded to build an IMDB Top 250 clone. We then improved on this model to build a knowledge-based recommender that took into account the recommended movies' genre, duration, and year of release.
- Next, we learned how to build content-based recommenders using plot lines and subsequently more sophisticated metadata, such as the genre, cast, crew, and keywords. In the process, we familiarized ourselves with vectorizers and the cosine similarity metric.
- In the chapter on data mining, we were introduced to the various techniques used in building and improving recommendation systems. We learned about similarity metrics other than the cosine score. We then proceeded to study clustering, with an emphasis on k-means clustering techniques. This was followed by discussions on dimensionality reduction (with an emphasis on PCA) and the various supervised learning techniques. The chapter concluded with a tour of evaluation metrics that are used to gauge the performance of recommender systems.

- The chapter on collaborative filtering had us experimenting with a variety of models that used rating data, and also leveraged data mining techniques introduced in the previous chapter. We were also introduced to the `surprise` library, which made building recommender systems a breeze.
- In this final chapter, we briefly discussed the various kinds of hybrid recommender used in the industry today and built a model that incorporated collaborative filtering into a content-based engine to offer personalized recommendations to a user, while keeping the current movie being watched in mind.

What we have covered, of course, only touches the surface of the world of recommender systems. However, I am positive that readers will now be in a very good place to tackle advanced topics in the field. I have listed a few resources in the `Appendix` that could serve as a next stop on your journey to becoming a recommendations master.

As mentioned earlier, all the code written as part of this book is available as a GitHub repository to enable you to effortlessly tinker and experiment with the code as you journey through this book. I'd like to thank you all for having come this far. If you have any comments, corrections, criticism, or suggestions, feel free to contact me at `rounakbanik@gmail.com`.

Other Books You May Enjoy

If you enjoyed this book, you may be interested in these other books by Packt:

Statistics for Machine Learning
Pratap Dangeti

ISBN: 9781788295758

- Understand the Statistical and Machine Learning fundamentals necessary to build models
- Understand the major differences and parallels between the statistical way and the Machine Learning way to solve problems
- Learn how to prepare data and feed models by using the appropriate Machine Learning algorithms from the more-than-adequate R and Python packages
- Analyze the results and tune the model appropriately to your own predictive goals
- Understand the concepts of required statistics for Machine Learning
- Introduce yourself to necessary fundamentals required for building supervised & unsupervised deep learning models
- Learn reinforcement learning and its application in the field of artificial intelligence domain

Feature Engineering Made Easy
Sinan Ozdemir, Divya Susarla

ISBN: 9781787287600

- Identify and leverage different feature types
- Clean features in data to improve predictive power
- Understand why and how to perform feature selection, and model error analysis
- Leverage domain knowledge to construct new features
- Deliver features based on mathematical insights
- Use machine-learning algorithms to construct features
- Master feature engineering and optimization
- Harness feature engineering for real world applications through a structured case study

Leave a review - let other readers know what you think

Please share your thoughts on this book with others by leaving a review on the site that you bought it from. If you purchased the book from Amazon, please leave us an honest review on this book's Amazon page. This is vital so that other potential readers can see and use your unbiased opinion to make purchasing decisions, we can understand what our customers think about our products, and our authors can see your feedback on the title that they have worked with Packt to create. It will only take a few minutes of your time, but is valuable to other potential customers, our authors, and Packt. Thank you!

Index

CPSIA information can be obtained
at www.ICGtesting.com
Printed in the USA
LVHW061239040922
727579LV00006B/440